WHAT THE BIBLE REALLY TELLS US

ADRIAN BENARD

INKS & BINDINGS

Inks and Bindings
888-290-5218
www.inksandbindings.com
orders@inksandbindings.com

CONTENTS

PREFACE

Who would want to write about an illusionary deity, particularly if he or she were born and raised in a religious environment where parents, school, and church constantly remind him or her of the all-forgiving, merciful, and beneficent deity? All through life it has been drummed into you that you cannot live without a heavenly father who protects you and grants your wishes through prayer, and if it does not come out according to expectations, then you are told that God works in mysterious ways! He always wins that way and never can be wrong because He knows what is good for you even if it does not appear that way—similar to St. Nick.

When I was a teenager, I asked many questions and was told to read the Bible, because all the answers were in there, and ask God for enlightenment. However, when I did read and ask for enlightenment and when I analyzed the Bible, more questions came up. I was then told not to read too much into it and not to take everything literally. My questions remained and were never satisfactorily answered. So, when still a teenager, I started to write down everything that could not be explained. I remained a devout Christian in my way because I figured, *What do I have to lose if I agree with what I am being indoctrinated in?*

You can ask the same question to different clergy, and you'll get a different answer from each one—or they will tell you nothing in so many words.

Churches are nice in the respect that everybody in a church believes in the same thing, supposedly, even if every church has different dogmas and beliefs but the same God. Churches are businesses—big business—if they cannot make money, they are out.

I was in France in the late forties and found in an old Bible there a little card that gave the owner of that card a guaranteed entry into heaven, but originally, he or she had to pay a price to acquire that privilege. This is just one example, and there are not too many churches nowadays that give free tickets to heaven for a price. The Roman Catholic Church did so many years ago and maybe still does—if the price, or the *donation*, is right.

Anyhow, this booklet is not written for you to read in bed before you go to sleep, though it may make you sleepy and drowsy enough to fall asleep. No, it needs an alert mind to analyze and comprehend what is written about the diverse subjects. And it is not a book to be read from A to Z in one sitting. It needs to be studied.

CHAPTER 1

Duplicate Gods

Anyone who is even a little bit familiar with the Bible knows that the very first verse is written as follows: "In the beginning God created the heaven and the earth." What not too many people know is that in the original manuscript, it is written, "In the beginning the Gods created the heavens and the earth."

However, it is never translated with the plural *Gods*. Why is that?

There are numerous references to the "Gods" in the Bible. We will look at this in a little while.

The scriptures that are being used are from the King James Version (Protestant), the Douay Confraternity and Vulgate (both Roman Catholic), and the New International Version (protestant).

Henceforth, when applicable, the following conventions are followed:

- The King James translation will be referred to as KJ.
- The Douay Confraternity will be referred to as DC.
- Which can not be quoted due to copy rights.
- The New International Version will be referred to as NIV.
- Also copy righted.
- The Hebrew Bible will be referred to as HB.

The original Hebrew Bible has been translated many times, by five or six different translators, and by many more people who all did their best in translating. Many of them were killed by the church, if the Vatican did not like their translations.

Originally the Hebrew Bible was translated into the Greek language and from there into the Latin versions. After that, there were again hundreds of translations made by diverse people, also clergy, around the Middle Ages, and all had good intentions, but some of them wrote translations that were not accepted by the Vatican, and those poor guys were murdered on the orders of the Vatican and their works burned. Then the translation to the King James Version happened, and many more translations came about after that. They are still being produced.

What happened with the latest Bible translations, called the New International Version, the Revised English Bible, the New International Bible, or whatever else? They took the original Bible, which is and was God's word, as it was accepted and originally written supposedly by God's inspiration.

The original Bible has been molested in the new translations to the extent that the majority of all the words and verses throughout the Bible have been changed. If you read the King James next to the New International Version, you will have a heck of a time trying to follow it. Sentences that cannot be explained as written and to the liking of the translators have their wording changed, and whole verses are changed just so it suits most of the Christian denominations.

This indicates God has to be corrected, because it seems God did not know what He was doing when the Bible was put together, even if it was all done by His inspiration.

Blasphemy is what it is, correcting His word, with all good intentions.

Some sayings by God or even Jesus have been changed, indicating that the people who are making the new translations supposedly knew better than God what it should say.

It is written in Revelation 22:19, "And if any man shall take away from the words of this book, God shall take away his part out of the book of life, and out of the holy city, and from the things written in this book."

As it states on the cover of the New English Bible (NEB), "Although it stands firmly in the tradition of the NEB, the extensive changes now made, and to the degree to which it has been enhanced ..."

Why do we need a new, extensively changed and enhanced Bible?

Is it because the original translation of the Bible, which is supposed to be God's word, was not good enough? All through the ages, it was good enough.

If it was only to change the "thee" and the "ye" and the "thou" and some more words that don't belong in our language anymore, that would make sense.

Have you ever heard of anybody trying to change or enhance the works of Shakespeare, for example, because they needed to be explained or enhanced? Or did anybody ever attempt to change the works of Edgar Allan Poe, Robert Shaw, or even the great composers like Beethoven and Mozart?

No, their work is and stays as finished, and nobody will touch it to change or enhance it. The Bible is God's word as it was originally written. Can we as humans improve on His word?

Who wrote the first five books in the Bible? According to religious history and theologians, it was Moses. He was raised for forty years and tutored in the Egyptian courts as an Egyptian and as the son of a pharaoh; that way, he became quite well versed and indoctrinated in the ways the Egyptians believed and in their way of living. He became, for instance, thoroughly familiar with the stars, the Egyptian Gods, and all their rituals. He obviously was not trained in the beliefs of his ancestors by the Egyptians.

Moses probably had no idea that he was an Israelite. But he had to flee from the Egyptians after taking the side of the Israelites. So he went to Sinai, and there he stayed for another forty years, living as a shepherd. He married while living there. His father-in-law was not all that helpful in training Moses either. He was the one who told him, "Now I know that the Lord God is greater than all Gods." Moses himself made that same statement later to the Lord God.

Now, all of a sudden, he was chosen by the God of Israel to become the leader and to help the Israelites get out of Egypt. He lived to be 120 years old. The first forty years he lived as an Egyptian and the next forty years as a shepherd, and the last forty years he spent in the desert. He had to have written the Pentateuch, the first five books of the Bible, while in the hot desert. Yes, he did. But he must have gotten the details of the story from Genesis to Deuteronomy mostly by hearsay.

And while being indoctrinated in Egypt for forty years, he could even write about his own death and some more events that happened after he died. Well, more about that later. Back to the beginning of the Bible and this book.

Every clergy worth his or her salt knows that it is written in the original Hebrew bible in the following way:

It says, in the beginning Elohim (the Gods) created the heavens and the earth.

Elohim is plural for Gods.

Eloha is a singular God.

Consequently, anywhere throughout the Old Testament where God is mentioned; then it means the Elohim God (the Gods).

As proof go to Gen 1:26, where in every bible it says; God said "Let us [the Gods] make men in our [the Gods] image in our [the Gods] likeness.

When I served at Cannon Air Force Base, I discussed this one day with a captain there. He told me I was full of it, because he had never heard that— just like the majority of Christian people. They also have not heard that, or they don't want to hear about it. We agreed he could call any clergy in town and ask him or her about it. He chose to call a Methodist preacher. His part of the telephone conversation went like this:

It does say so? How come I never heard of this?

When the conversation was over, he gave me a puzzled look, like he was lost, while shrugging his shoulders. Then, without saying anything, he went back to his office. So, I never heard the answer. But so be it.

We can prove that the plural form is not used in the manner for royalty, like in the olden days, as in "we" for the king of England. Then royalty was used in plurality. Besides, this plurality in the English language had nothing to do with the creation of the Bible, and most of the countries that had kingdoms did not use this expression. Only in England was it used.

Also, it is not feasible to look at it as representing the Trinity, because the Trinity came about when the first pope after Peter put out an edict that from then on, God, His son, and the Holy Spirit would be looked upon not as three Gods but as only one God.

This was done by the first pope who reigned after Christ's existence—again, not to be confused with Peter, who is also referred to as the first pope. So, the Trinity did not exist in the Old Testament, and the Trinity was never mentioned by God or Jesus! The original pope did not call them a trinity either. However, the Bible, in some instances, makes references to the father and the son being the same, but never as a trinity, per se.

Neither God nor Jesus nor the Holy Spirit ever proclaimed that they were part of a trinity. By the way, the Holy Spirit never made any statements according to the Bible.

The original pope, who was the emperor of Constantinople, told the other religious leaders, they had to many Gods, like the Roman Gods, the Greek Gods, the Scandinavian Gods, the Indian Gods, the Egyptian Gods, and so on.

However, they rebutted his argument with "You have three gods yourself— that is, God, the Son, and the Holy Spirit." They caught him with his pants down, so to speak. And they were right!

Consequently, he made the edict that henceforth the three deities would be looked upon as one God. How convenient. And later, in the year 325 at the Council of Nicene, this creed became an agreement with the clergy. Fifty-six years later, in 381, it was adopted at the next council of Constantinople and became the standard creed of the Catholic Church. Later it was also adopted by almost all Protestant denominations, except for the Universal Church and a few other denominations, who did not believe in the Trinity. They were persecuted and killed on orders from the Vatican! Many of them fled to Poland and Holland in the Middle Ages, and most of them were killed if they did not believe in the Trinity—again, on orders from the Vatican.

Let's face it; there is more than one God. Let's look at a few.

First, we have to look at the name *God*. *God* is a generic name; this means that all deities, wherever they might be, are named God.

God

Everybody knows and is familiar with the Christian "God." This is the God all Christians believe in.

No matter which denomination—and there are quite a few Protestant denominations, sects, and cults—they all believe in the same God; however, each one's followers think they alone have the right religion for salvation. They never like a different church because there are too many things wrong with those other churches, like their dogmas and creeds. They profess according to them and believe the only right church for salvation is the one they belong to! So why are there so many different churches? They all believe in the same God, Jesus the Christ, and Satan.

This indicates churches are big business. Like the Roman Catholic Church, the Church of Latter-Day Saints, the Baptist Church, Scientology, and some other large, created churches. I am not talking about the smaller ones. Most of those preachers can barely scrape by.

Muslims know God, and at least they gave Him the name *Allah* instead of the generic name *God*. And he is the Supreme Being for them.

The Hindus also have their Gods but have different names for them obviously. So do other religions.

All over the world, the name *God* is used when swearing, as in "God damn!" or when one is surprised, then it is used as "God Almighty!" or "Oh my God!"—even when God told everybody in one of His Ten Commandments, "You shall not use my name in vain." But what was his name? According to the Hebrew Bible, it was not *God*, but *Elohim* and obviously not *Yahweh* because this could not be pronounced.

God mentioned *Ishi*. Yes, He wanted to be called Ishi and not anymore Baali. This will be discussed later in this chapter.

God

But where He came from is something else.

In the Hebrew Bible, God is known as *Elohim* or the *Holy One*. And the Lord or Lord God with a name that nobody was allowed to say became known as Jaweh or as the *most* Holy one.

In the Bible, it is written literally as follows:

"God came from Teman and the Holy one from mount Paran" (Habakkuk 3:3).

Here, we have two Gods living in different locations in Israel!

God does not come from heaven? No, sir, He came from Teman. Anyhow, we have here two distinct, different Gods:

1. God, the Holy One
2. The Most Holy One.

That sounds almost like saying John is from New York and Harry from Chicago. Teman is a city close to Edom. This still does not tell us much. Is wisdom no more in Teman? (2 Jeremiah 49:20).

If God came from Teman and the Holy one from Paran, then maybe they had a summer residence there? Regardless, they are identified as two different Gods: God and the Holy One!

The Holy One lived on Mount Paran.

In Genesis 21:21, it is stated, "And he dwelt in the wilderness of Paran." The Bible talks here about the son of Hagar. Hagar was Abraham's substitute wife. She was the maid of his wife, and his wife wanted him to have sex with her just to produce offspring. Abraham did get a child by Hagar, and he became the father of Hagar's son, who was named Ishmael. He was involved with the Islamic religion.

Abraham's wife, Sarah, could not produce a child, so she wanted her husband to have a child with Hagar her maid. And he did have a child with her. This part of the Bible and other similar occasions do not say much about the matter of matrimony, like the NIV version and others like to talk about. But in those days, it seems it was common.

Paran does not sound like much of a place for a God—a mountain and a wilderness?

Well, did He not supposedly create this wilderness and mountain Himself?

Again, in Samuel 25:1, we read, "And David arose and went down to the wilderness in Paran." Why? To hunt maybe or to communicate with the Holy One in Paran?

We are talking here about two different deities—two Gods who resided in two different locations, one in Teman and the other in Paran!

Leviticus 21: 22, "He shall eat the bread of his God, *both* of the most holy, and of the holy one" (emphasis added). Again, the mentioning of the two different deities!

1. The Holy One
2. The Most Holy

Now we have to look at the printed word in the Bible. Every time there is a reference to a heathen or a strange or foreign God, it is printed as *god* with a small *g*. When the Christian God is mentioned, it is printed as *God* with a capital "G." This was pointed out to me by a friend of mine, and he sure did make an excellent point here as far as the Bible shows.

However, when God or the priests told the Israelites not to serve different Gods, how did they pronounce "God" with a capital "G" or a small "g"? There is no distinction like that in speech!

So, it is the writers of the Bible's books who decided to make the difference by writing "God" with a "G."

The Lord, the Lord God

The Lord, the Lord God, merciful and gracious, long suffering and abundant in truth. Keeping mercy for thousands, forgiving iniquity [wickedness] and transgressions and sin; visiting the iniquity [wickedness] of the fathers upon the children, and upon the children's children, unto the third and fourth generation. (Exodus 34:6–7; see also Exodus 20:5, Deuteronomy 5:9 and 4:31, and Numbers 14:18)

This sure does not sound much like a merciful Lord when you analyze these passages!

If one gets a child who is born in a pitiful state, like completely dependent on his or her parents, in other words, being a vegetable, or a baby born blind, malformed, mentally challenged, or whatever, then you can blame that on the iniquity of the baby's grandfather or the baby's great-grandfather. But the child is innocent and has to suffer for the sins of the grandfather, the great- grandfather, or the great-great-grandfather who lived up to three or four generations back. Not much of a merciful and righteous God! How He can justify that is beyond me, particularly when He proclaimed, "I keep mercy for thousands, *forgiving iniquity*, merciful, and gracious."

However, when "but" comes up, this means everything previous to it is cancelled.

According to the dictionary, *but* ranges in meaning from the faintest contrast to absolute negation.

We continue, " ... but visiting *the iniquity* of the fathers upon the children, and the children's children. Up to the third and fourth generation"

So not only the innocent children but also their children and their children's children and so on are being punished for the sins of the forefathers for up to four generations.

Even the parents who have punished children, those parents will have to suffer too, all because of their forefathers. How can God Almighty let innocent children and their parents suffer so much? It is incomprehensible.

It certainly looks like the Lord's concern is only for men. He does not care much about babies or, for that matter, not all that much for women and animals either, except when animals are offered to Him on an altar. Then He savors the smell of meat. It seems babies, little children, and animals don't count much by the Lord!

He brings up the same warning in the Bible *four more times*, so just hope your grandfather or great-grandfather did not sin, so your babies are not born to suffer, along with their parents.

Couldn't the Lord punish the sinners themselves instead of the children? No, only the children. Generations later, they have to suffer. How awful!

Jeremiah 31:34 states, "Know the Lord, for they shall all know me, says the Lord, for I will forgive their iniquity and I will remember their sin no more." Here He contradicts Himself. This we don't expect from God, who is not supposed to allege or make contradictions. Look at what He said about the previously mentioned iniquities in 2 Chronicles 25:4: "As it is written in the law in the book of Moses, where the Lord said: The fathers shall not die for the children: *neither shall the children die for the fathers, but every man for his own sin.*" This makes sense, but again, what about all the children who died because of their forefathers in the previously mentioned texts?

The two verses in the preceding paragraph make more sense than what the Lord said earlier, that the children had to suffer for the sins of their forefathers, but what does it mean? Here, the Lord gives conflicting stories. And contradictions galore!

In Jeremiah 32:18, Jeremiah is praying to God, and he says, "You showed loving kindness to thousands, and recompensed the iniquity of the fathers to the bosom of their children after them; the great mighty God, the Lord of hosts is his name."

It sure sounds here that Jeremiah is just patronizing the Lord. Maybe he got some brownie points for saying that.

Lamentations 5:7 says, "Our fathers have sinned, and are not, and we have borne their iniquity."

Here we go again, one conflicting story after the other. So which is it? Is he punishing the children here again? It shows a God who is wishy-washy. Well, enough of the sins and the contradictions He blatantly shows throughout the Bible.

Exodus 20:5 says, "I the Lord thy God am a jealous God."

Exodus 34:14 says, "For thou shall worship no other God; for the Lord *whose name* is Jealous, is a jealous God"

Here we have another one. At least here God has a name. Yes, this God is called jealous, and He is jealous for sure. It says here "whose *name* is jealous," not Ishi or Baali.

Deuteronomy 4:24 says, "For the Lord thy God is a consuming fire, even a jealous God."

Deuteronomy 32:21 states, "They have moved me to jealousy with that which is not God."

Again, a God who is jealous?

11

"While he was zealous for my sake [the Lord's sake] among them, that I consumed not the children of Israel in my jealousy" (Numbers 25:11).

So, he is jealous of other Gods, and He does not care at all about other foreign or heathen Gods. He hates them with a passion, and He cannot do anything about this? He definitely has no use for those Gods for any reason. So, it seems He is powerless as far as the strange Gods are concerned. The only thing He can be is jealous.

Deuteronomy 6:14–15 reads, "Ye shall not go after other gods, of the gods of the people who are round about you. For the Lord your God is a jealous God among you lest the anger of the Lord destroy thee from of the face of the earth."

Here we have a threat, just because He is a jealous God. How absurd!

Exodus 33:13 says, " … and make no mention of the name of other Gods, neither let it be heard out of your mouth."

And Exodus 23:24 says, "You shall not bow down to their gods, nor serve them nor do after their works."

Joshua 24: 19 states, "And Joshua said to the people: 'You cannot serve the Lord: for He is a holy God; He is a jealous God; He will not forgive your transgressions or your sins.'"

A few paragraphs ago, we talked about how God stated, "I will forgive iniquities and transgressions."

Besides the last verse makes *no* sense, when Joshua says, "You cannot serve the Lord for He is a Holy and a jealous God."

Well, we continue with God proclaiming that He is a jealous God. That does not say much for that God. He is jealous of other Gods, so He said. It certainly is not very godly, being jealous or envious.

Throughout the Old Testament, the Gods kept on harping on and on about strange or foreign Gods and to stay away from them. It seems this is one of the most vexing problems for the Gods! The Gods are worried that the Israelites might like foreign Gods better, as they did many times. Because all around the Israelites were foreign

Gods and they were being worshipped by all kinds of people. So, it rubbed off time after time. Why couldn't God just ignore all those foreign Gods? They must have been a real threat to Him!

The Lord is a God who is vindictive and always ready to punish if things are not going His way. And from all indications, the strange Gods definitely must have been friendlier Gods, nicer and more tolerant than the Gods of the Israelites.

During the forty-year trek through the desert after they came out of Egypt, they made a calf out of gold and worshipped it. This episode ticked off the Lord something fierce. At first, He was going to destroy *all the Israelites*, so He said! However, Moses managed to talk Him out of it.

Besides that, there are many more instances where the Israelites worshipped foreign Gods all through the Bible. And God kept threatening the Israelites throughout the Old Testament by telling them more than 150 times that if they did, there would be dire consequences. Because He is a jealous God!

Leviticus 19:4 warns, "Turn ye not to idols, nor molten Gods."

God Almighty

"God said to Moses: I am the Lord and I appeared unto Abraham, unto Isaac, and unto Jacob, by the name of God almighty, but by my name Jehovah, was I not known to them" (Exodus 6:3).

Here we have the Lord or God Almighty and Jehovah (Jahweh) being one and the same. So be it.

But in Exodus 22:14, we read, "And Abraham called the name of the altar on which he was ready to offer his son: 'Jehovah–jireh.'" But "by my name Jehovah was I not known to Abraham," according to God. How strange that Abraham still used the name *Jehovah*. In other words, Abraham, *according to the Gods*, did not know anything about Jehovah! He supposedly never heard of Him either. However, he still named an altar after the God Jehovah! "Jehova-jireh." In spite of supposedly not knowing Jehovah and being unaware that there was a God by the name of Jehovah! How strange!

Abraham could not have picked a name like Jehovah out of thin air, because he named the altar after a God and Jehovah was a very holy name. Here the Lord Himself did not know that Abraham was well aware of the name Jehovah, in spite of Him saying, "I was not known to Abraham by my name Jehovah." Strange, to say the least, and again contradictory!

The Most High God

Genesis 14:18 says, "And he was the priest of the most high God."

This is the highest God of all the Gods. In other words, He must be the head honcho.

Genesis 14:19–20 says, "Blessed be Abram of the most high God. And blessed be the most high God."

Genesis 14:22 continues, "Abram said: I have lift up mine hand to *the Lord*, the most high God."

If we have a most high God, then there must be a high God also. And we know there is more than one God.

A God

In Genesis 17:7, we read, "And I will be to you *a God*." This is God talking to Moses.

He did not say, "I will be God to you," or "I will be the God to you." No, He said, "a God." Was this a slip of the tongue? Gods, as a rule, don't say the wrong thing. That's why they are supposed to be Gods.

So again, here we have a God, but which one? Maybe in the next new Bible translations, they still have a chance to change this in the future too.

Even Moses talks about plural Gods, and he knows that there is more than one God, just like all the Gods the Egyptians worshipped. The Israelites too were familiar with all those Gods.

Joshua 24:14 says, "Now therefore fear the Lord, and serve him in sincerity and put away the Gods which your fathers served on the other side of the flood and in Egypt."

This indicates that the Israelites also knew and worshipped quite a few Gods at the time when they were in Egypt and they did adore them too.

The Most Holy and the Holy

In Leviticus 21:22, we read, "He shall eat the bread of his God, both of the most holy and of the Holy."

Again, here we have two distinct, different Gods. We do know the Holy One from earlier, remember? He is the one from Mount Paran.

Now We Come to Ishi

Hosea 2:16 says, "Said the Lord, you shall call me Ishi and no more Baali" (KJ)

It becomes obvious, because *Baali* is too close to the heathen God's named Baal, Baal-Berith, Baalim, Baale, Baal-Gad, Baal-Hazor, Baal-Hermon, Baal- Meon, and a few more of the Gods named Baal-Peor, Baal-Peratim, Baal- Shalisha, and Baal-Tamar. So there were numerous foreign Gods with a name close to Baali.

Judges 9:33 says, "As soon as Gideon was dead the children of Israel turned again, and went a whoring after Baalim, and made Baal-berith their god."

No wonder God got jealous of all those Gods! So, Baali (which was God's name) created confusion with all those strange Gods that had similar names as the Israelite's God, we can observe.

Not too many people are familiar with those names. At least here, the Lord had a real name, Ishi, which did not stick. The Lord would have had a real name if they had just followed the Lord's instructions. We would still have been praying to O Great Ishi.

Baali

Don't call me Baali anymore; just call me *Ishi*.

Did the Israelites call God "<u>Baali</u>"? Obviously, they must have! According to God, they did. So now He wants them to call Him "<u>Ishi</u>." It must not have happened, because we never hear about that name anymore. Did God say it on a whim? Or maybe it is completely missing from the Bible? Or is it ignored? It is only mentioned a few times in Chronicles 2 that the sons of Israel had sons born to them and they named them Ishi.

I Am That I Am

In Exodus 3:14, Moses is talking to the Lord, "When I say to the children of Israel, The *God of your fathers* has sent me, then they shall say, his name is what?" This indicates that the Israelites knew many Gods. So, they wanted to know the name of the God of their fathers.

And again, in Joshua 24:14, it says, "Now therefore fear the Lord, and serve him in sincerity and put away the Gods which your fathers served on the other side of the flood, and in Egypt." So, this indicates the Israelites did know at the time quite a few Gods when they resided in Egypt.

In other words, who are those Gods, He is talking about? Holy mackerel! Moses anticipated that the people of Israel needed more than that, because he figured, "the God of your fathers" did not ring a bell with the Israelites as he was raised in Egypt. So, he should know.

"So, the Lord said to Moses, tell them *I Am That I Am*, and tell them, *I Am* has sent me to you" (Exodus 3:14).

It sounds like God is getting aggravated. Now, He says, "As a matter of fact, just tell them, *I Am* has sent me to you." This would have been very ineffective for Moses to tell the Israelites.

The Israelites probably would have said, "*I Am*? Never heard of that one."

With all the names floating around, why not one of those names: God Almighty, Most High God, Jehovah, Ishi, or Baali? Any one of those names might have rung a bell.

Well, *I Am* is not an issue anymore and does not appear any more in the Bible, so this was used only once, in this instance, just like *Ishi* and *Baali*. Either the Israelites did not even know who the God of their fathers was, or Moses worried too much. However, the Lord must have realized the mistake He almost made. Now the Lord changes His mind, just like a human being, and continues, "Thus shall you say to the children of Israel: the Lord God of your fathers, The God of Abraham, the God of Isaac, and the God of Jacob, has sent me to you."

Observe, God does *not* say, "the God of Abraham, Isaac, and Jacob." No, now it does give the impression to the Israelites that there are three different Gods: the God of Abraham, the God of Isaac, and the God of Jacob, each his own God?

In Exodus 6:3, He continues, "And I appeared to Abraham and to Isaac and to Jacob, by the name of God almighty." Again a change!

Now the Lord comes again when He said to Moses in Exodus 6:6, "Say to the children of Israel, *I am the Lord*. And I will be to you a God: and you shall know that I am the Lord your God."

It seems here the Lord cannot quite make up His mind. After telling Moses to tell the Israelites that the "I am" had sent him to them. He changed his mind again and told Moses, "thus shall you say to the children of Israel, "The Lord God of your fathers, the God of Abraham, the God of Isaac and the God of Jacob, has sent me to you."

If that was not enough, in Exodus 6:7, He changed his mind again. This time, He said to Moses, "Say to the children of Israel, I am the Lord. And I will be to you a God; and you shall know that I am the Lord your God."

It's very confusing, to say the least, for Moses and the Israelites. The poor guy had to tell the Israelites all of the following:

1. The "I am that I am" has sent me, or the "I am" has sent me.
2. "The God of Abraham and the God of Isaac and the God of Jacob" has sent me.
3. "God almighty" has sent me.
4. "The Lord and I will bring you out of Egypt" (Exodus 6:7).
5. "I will be to you a God." (That's for sure, but which one?)
6. "And you shall know that I am the Lord your God."

He had plenty of names for the Israelites, and then He also said, "I will be to you a God—not God, but "a God." In other words, He will be one of the Gods.

Now the Israelites must have thought, *Holy mackerel, how many Gods are getting us out of Egypt?*

Isaiah 42:8 says, "I am the Lord: that is my name. And my glory will I not give to another, neither my praise to graven images."

Deuteronomy 10:17 says, "For the Lord your Lord God is God of Gods and of Lords."

What do we have here? God admits He is one of many! If God says that He is *the God of Gods*, then this would mean that He is the God over all Gods, foreign Gods and Hebrew Gods; besides that, He admits there are other Gods and not just Him. There never is a reference to foreign Lords, so He is the Lord of Lords.

Surely that is what He means, because interestingly, the Lord God Himself gives the command "You shall not revile the Gods!" (KJ) Exodus 22:28.

Here God does not have any qualms saying, "You shall not revile the Gods."

Observe, the Lord God says "the Gods." The Lord God does not leave any doubt that there are other Gods existing besides him. He states here clearly, that there are multiple Gods!

And the Lord God nevertheless gives His command *not to vilify or abuse any of those Gods.*

Why does He have mercy, and why does He suddenly feel respectful of all of those strange Gods, if He is talking about strange Gods? This only works if He is talking about other Gods like Himself, because He has no use for and dislikes foreign Gods with a passion. Remember He is jealous of them, so He would never say anything respectful or nice about other Gods! This indicates God always feels threatened by strange Gods. And surely, we have more than one God here, as He made clear by saying, "You shall not revile the Gods."

The Lord God Himself gives the command:

"You shall revile the gods" (KJ) Exodus 22:28.

Here we go again in the NIV; they changed God's word so it conveniently falls into place for them by making the Gods a singular God. This indicates God made a mistake in giving us His "Word," the Bible. Now it looks like God did not know what He was doing? The change from Gods to God is also a glaring one.

Deuteronomy 10:17 reads,

"The Lord God of Gods, the Lord God of Gods" (KJ).

He is the *mightiest God.* That is what the children of Reuben and of Gad and of Manasseh said unto the heads of the thousands of Israel. He knows, and Israel He shall know.

So, He says He is above all Gods. But why does He even mention all the other Gods. If He proclaims Himself to be the Lord God and the mightiest God, then He sets himself up to be better than God in Joshua 22:29.

1) "God forbid that we should rebel against the Lord" (KJ).

Here *God* Himself gives the order not to go against *the Lord.* Absolutely two different Gods!

Among the Gods

Moses here makes the statement, "Who is like unto thee, O Lord, among the Gods?" (Exodus 15:12).

Here, Moses talks about "Gods," plural. He knows that there is more than one God. Why? He was familiar with all those Egyptian Gods! Again, Moses compares God to all the other Gods.

Exodus 18:11 says, "Now I know that *the Lord God is greater than all Gods:* for in the thing wherein they dealt proudly He was above them." Thus said Moses's father-in-law to Moses.

In 2 Chronicles 2:5, we read, "For great is our God above all Gods. And the house, which I build is great; for great is our God above all Gods."

This is what King Solomon proclaimed when building the temple. Even Solomon admits there are other Gods besides God.

Psalm 82:1 says the following:

• "He judged among the gods" (KJ).

God stood *in the congregation of the mighty*. He judged among the Gods. If *those Gods stood in the assembly of the mighty*, which certainly are all Gods, how else could He judge among the Gods? He either admits and recognizes that there are other existing Gods, heathen or regular Gods, or He is incoherent.

If those Gods are strange Gods, why would He have to judge them? He abhors strange Gods. This mean there are strange Gods and those strange Gods are in the assembly of the mighty also. Then this would mean that the strange Gods are mighty also. So it sure looks like *God did judge among the Gods*!

Psalm 97:9 says, "Thou are exalted far above all Gods. For thou, Lord, are high above all earth: thou are exalted far above all Gods." Here we go again.

Psalm 135:5 says, "Our Lord is above all Gods. For I know that the Lord is great, and that our Lord is above all Gods." Why does the Lord have to keep bringing up that He is above all Gods, if He does not recognize any God besides Himself? Is He getting paranoid? This means there are other Gods! In the Trinity, He is the same as God. But now He is above Gods.

In Daniel 2:37, it says, "Your God is a God of Gods. Of a truth it is that your God is *a God of Gods*." Here King Nebuchadnezzar is speaking to Daniel.

Job 1:6 and Job 2:1 say, "And the sons of God came to present themselves to the Lord."

Here we have an undeniable fact that the *sons of God* presented themselves to *the Lord* and not to their father, which is God, they being sons of God. It is another indication of two Gods. Otherwise, it would have been written, "And the sons of God came to present themselves to their father or to God." No, it says distinctly "to the Lord."

The God of Gods

Psalm 136:2 reads, "O, give thanks to the God of Gods." In the next verse, it states, "O give thanks to the Lord of Lords." Every time, supposedly, the foreign Gods are being mentioned as if they also coexist. Then there must be other Gods. Of all the foreign Gods, God is the God? God does not want to be a God over foreign Gods! He is still jealous about strange Gods.

Genesis 1:26 has more about Gods. "And God said: 'let us make man in *our* image, after *our* likeness'"—plural Gods.

Genesis 3:22 says, "And the Lord God said: 'behold the man is become as one of us'"—plural "Gods."

Genesis 11:7 states, "And the Lord said: 'go to let us go down, and there confound their language'"

Genesis 3:8 also indicates more than one God. "And Adam and his woman heard the voice of the Lord God walking in the garden." It's very doubtful that God was singing or muttering or talking to Himself so again, plural Gods!

In Genesis 6:19, God tells Noah to take two of each of the animals.

In Genesis 7:2, the Lord tells Noah to take of the clean beasts by sevens. The Lord is also talking about clean beasts! This was not in existence, until much later, when God instructed Moses to tell the Israelites about the clean and unclean animals.

God and the Lord are two different entities. Both the Lord and God give conflicting commands to Noah. If they are not two different Gods, then God would be utterly confused and incoherent.

The following names of God are all names out of the Jewish Bible and used to refer to God.

- *Elohim* is another name for God and is also a plural form; it comes from *Eloah*.
- *Adonai* is one of several names for God and is plural; the basic form is *Adonah*.
- *Ad El-Shaddai* translates as "God Almighty."
- Other names are *Jaweh*, *Jehovah*, and *Jah*, which is short for *Jehovah*.

Kabbalah is a Jewish mystical interpretation of the Bible. In the Kabbalah, it states that there are seventy-two names for God—or maybe seventy-two Gods? And in the Torah, the Jewish Bible, there are ten names for God listed.

The following are some more Jehovahs whose names are synonymous with the altars that were built for them.

1. *Jehovah-Nisse* is the name of an altar built by Moses to honor
2. the God Jehovah-Nisse.
3. *Jehovah-Jireh* is the name of an altar built by Abraham when he was tem by God to offer his son on an altar. The altar was built in honor of the Jehovah-Jireh—in spite of Abraham not knowing Jehovah, according to
4. *Jehovah-shalom* is the name of an altar built by Gideon to honor
5. the God Jehovah-Shalom.

Some more Gods are mentioned here

I am convinced by analyzing the Bible that it can and has been proven that there are multiple Gods working together and at times do interfere with each other. The most obvious instances are when God himself says in Deuteronomi 10:17 "For the Lord your God is God of Gods and Lord of Lords." God never wants to associate Himself with foreign Gods, thus He must be the God of Gods (Elohim).

In Exodus 22:28, the command is given by God himself that "you shall not revile the gods!" This is straightforward and to the point. Here, God Himself makes it clear that there are multiple Gods and you shall not revile those Gods; in other words, do not vilify, abuse, or use abusive or contemptuous language toward them. That is only if they are foreign Gods? But nowhere in the Bible is there a reference where God is respectful of foreign Gods! He abhors them. So, God must be talking here about real Gods (Elohim)!

Genesis 7:1 tells of one place where they interfered with each other. God says to Noah to take *two of each* in the ark, and *the Lord* tells Noah to take clean beasts by **sevens** in the ark. And approximately 1,600 years later, God told Moses about the clean animals for the first time ever! So, Noah at his time could not have known what clean animals were!

After God told Noah to put *two* of each in the ark, "Then did Noah; according to all that God commanded him, so did he" (Genesis 6:22).

Now the Lord told Noah to take **seven** of every clean beast in the ark. "Then Noah did according unto all that the Lord commanded him" (Genesis 7:5). How could Noah have obeyed those two conflicting commands?

Well, enough about the Gods. There are more instances where the Gods are mentioned in plurality or duality all through the Old Testament. But enough is enough.

CHAPTER 2

The Two Gods—God and the Lord God

As I said earlier, in chapter 1, *God* is a generic name. Most deities in the whole wide world are named God.

Now it can be proven that the Christian God is great and good for everybody who wants to accept Him. It is quite a different story when we look at the Lord, who is also known as the Lord God. The Lord comes across as brutal. Everything has to be done His way or else. He made hundreds of laws, which probably made sense at the time when given, but most of those laws don't make sense anymore and are not followed nowadays.

The two Gods are also known in the He brew Bible by the following:

1) *Elohim*, who is God, is also plural, meaning "Gods."
2) *Jahweh* is the Lord or the Lord God.

Throughout the whole Bible, the actions of God and the Lord are intermingled. The Lord God is not to be confused with the Lord Jesus. It sure becomes obvious when we see all through the Bible that there is the mentioning of "God" as well as "the Lord" and "Lord God" and that those two entities are actually two distinct Gods. Now religion likes to proclaim that they are the same. To prove they are not the same, evidence will follow.

As mentioned earlier, the first line in the Bible, according to the original manuscripts and almost every clergy who went to a theological school, is written as follows: "In the beginning the Gods created the heavens and the earth." By analyzing the Bible, one can see they are the continuously mentioned over and over, *God* and the *Lord*. At times, He also wants to be called the Lord God. In other words, He also wants to be known as a God.

The whole first chapter in Genesis is done by God. He made the whole and complete creation. Now, in chapter 2, the Lord God comes in the picture. He wants to be known as the Lord God, because he also wants to be known as a God. He is also known as the Most High God. This indicates He wants to have the final say in every event and decision whatsoever. In other words, He wants to be the head honcho.

Now, occasionally, there will be repetition from chapter 1 to help make my point.

In Genesis 1:26, we look at God, where He made the statement as follows: "And God said let us make man in our image, after our likeness." Here we can assume that He is talking about himself.

In Genesis 2:4, it seems the Lord wants to do it better than God and starts the creation again! "In the day that the Lord God made the earth and the heavens, He even made the earth again! This means there must have been at one time two earths.

Genesis 2:5 continues, "And every plant before it was in the earth and every herb of the field before it grew: for the Lord God had not caused it to rain upon the earth." How is that? Every herb grew, but He had not caused it to rain. But it grew anyway?

Genesis 2:7 says, "And the Lord God formed man of the dust of the ground, and breathed in to his nostrils the breath of life, and man became a living soul." So now we have two men created? And the Lord put the man He had made in the Garden of Eden.

In Genesis 2:17, we read, "Now the Lord God gives the command to the man: you shall not eat from the tree of the knowledge of good and evil."

And Genesis 2:19 continues, "And the Lord God formed every beast of the field and fowls again and brought them to Adam to see what he would call them." This shows that the Lord God did not have any idea what Adam would call them. If God had known, then He would not have asked Adam. He had to see what the result was going to be. What was Adam going to call them? Not all that smart of the Lord God, because we normally say He is an all-knowing Lord God. He is omniscient.

Ezekiel 11:5 says, "I know the things that come into your mind, every one of them." Now this is a contradictory statement. If He knew, then the Lord did not have to bring every beast to Adam to see what he would call them. This indicates the Lord did not know what Adam was going to name them. If He knew everything that is in our minds, He would not have to ask, because He would know it already.

Then the Lord God took a rib from Adam and made a woman from that rib.

Genesis 3:1 says, "Now the serpent was more subtle than any beast of the field which the Lord God had made." So now we see that the Lord God also created the serpent.

Now, temporarily, God is out of the picture again. It is the Lord who is doing all the talking.

Again, in Genesis 2:17, we read, "The Lord God commanded the man, saying 'For in the day you eat there of you shall surely die." And the serpent said to the woman, "When you eat from that tree you shall not surely die." And he was right! We all know that they did not die the same day. So, the Lord made a threat He could not and did not enforce. So, Satan, if it was Satan, knew that Gods made empty threats.

Genesis 3:5 says, "The serpent said: 'for God knows that in the day you eat thereof, then your eyes shall be opened, and you shall be as gods, knowing good and evil." God Himself had named the tree "the tree of knowledge of good and evil."

Genesis 1:22 reads, "And the Lord God said: 'behold, the man is become as one of us, to know good and evil'" Thus, so far, the serpent had not lied.

In Matthew 10:16, Christ Himself makes the statement, "Be ye therefore wise as serpents."

The serpent was not a snake yet when they ate the forbidden fruit.

It was the Lord God who was walking in the garden and looking for Adam after he and his woman had eaten from the forbidden tree.

And when He called Adam, Adam said, "We heard your voice in the garden." What was he hearing? Was the Lord singing maybe or possibly muttering to Himself? No, sir, it is obviously the Lord was in a conversation with Gods!

He interrogated Adam and his woman. And the Lord God started cursing. A God who cursed! The Lord punished Adam, his woman, and the serpent. And the Lord God sent them forth from the Garden of Eden.

So, we see the Lord God was quite active during the fall of Adam and his woman, as Eve was never in the Garden of Eden—at least not by that name. Because when they were out of the Garden of Eden, then Adam gave her the name Eve (see Genesis 3:20).

In the story of Cain and Abel, it is the Lord again who handles everything. Now we come to the story of Noah. Here God complains about humankind. Noah found grace in the eyes of the Lord. So, He was the one who picked Noah.

It does not say who gave the instructions for Noah to build the ark or who gave the dimensions to build it. However, that sure was a fiasco when Noah had to put only one window in the ark. Not much fresh air circulation from a window of one-and-half-by-one-and-a-half foot in the ark for more than a year.

In Genesis 6:19 and 20, observe: it is God who tells Noah to take two of every sort of animal into the ark—male and female.

In Genesis 7:2, here comes the Lord again. He supposedly knows it better. He gives the command, "Put in the ark seven of the clean animals each, and two of the unclean animals." First God told Noah to take two of each animal and then the Lord told Noah to take seven of each animal.

If and only if God and the Lord are the same, we can see for sure that He does not know what He is talking about, meaning He is incoherent! So the two Gods can never be one God; they have to be two different deities!

Anyhow, it sure must have been confusing for Noah when the Lord was telling him to put seven of the animals in the ark—and clean ones to boot.

In Leviticus 11, Moses and Aaron, still in the desert, told all the Israelites, on orders of the Lord Himself, more than six hundred years after Noah's time, which animals were clean and they could eat from then on. They were also told which were unclean animals that they could not eat anymore. So Noah could not have known what a *clean* animal was.

Poor Noah, he probably got the impression that he had to give them a bath first to get them all clean.

"And God made a covenant with Noah, and He said; two of each shall you bring in the ark." Finally, two was the order and not seven.

Genesis 6:22 says, "Thus did Noah, according to all that God commanded him, so did he!"

Now here comes the Lord, and He said, "Of every clean beast you shall take by sevens and unclean by twos."

Genesis 7:5 says, "And Noah did, according to all that the Lord commanded him." Did he? This is contradictory to what was said earlier. "Then he did according to what God commanded him." Noah never boarded seven of the clean animals because he had already done what God commanded him earlier. Again, conflicting stories one after another.

Genesis 7:7 reads, "And Noah and his whole family went into the ark, because of the waters of the flood.

Genesis 7:8 mentions clean beasts and unclean beasts. This is impossible, because Noah had already done according to what God commanded him earlier. This was to take two of every sort.

Genesis 6:22 says, "Thus did Noah, according to all what God commanded him, so did he." So, the Lord tried to override God—with the seven of each and the clean and unclean beasts.

Genesis 7:9 says, "And now there went in two and two to Noah in the ark as God had commanded Noah." Regardless of clean and unclean beasts, they went into the ark two by two. This was the second time they went into the ark!

Genesis 7:12–13 reads, "And the rain was upon the earth forty days and nights. In the selfsame day entered Noah and his family into the ark." This was the third time they went into the ark.

Genesis 7:16 says, "And they that went into the ark, male and female of all flesh, as God had commanded him, and the Lord shut him in." They went in again for the fourth time. Strange, to say the least.

Well, the final result was that at the end, Noah put in two of each animal as God commanded him and the Lord shut him in. So the two, God and the Lord, were working together for a change—even if the Lord had to have the last word. However, it shows again there are two different entities at work here!

From then on, it was God who kept an eye on Noah, because at the end, He remembered them in the ark.

When they finally debarked, Noah built an altar for the Lord and took of every clean beast and of every *clean fowl* and offered burnt offerings on the altar. How did Noah know what a clean beast was? Noah took only two of every beast, regardless of whether they were clean or not. So, if they did not procreate, he wiped out a lot of species.

Did he use wood for the fire? Where would Noah have found wood? The ark would have been the only logical place to get it. And how did they get fire for the altar?

"And the lord smelled a sweet savor" (Genesis 8:21), as He always does when an offering is made.

Again, how did Noah know what a clean beast was? He did not put seven of each clean beast in the ark, as the Lord wanted him to do. No, Noah put two of the same kind of each animal, a male and a female, in the ark as God commanded him. So, what did Noah really do in those contradictory events?

This shows the Lord was interfering with God, because He wanted to have the last word. From then on, again, God kept an eye on Noah and told him what to eat. Now God told him he could eat every animal except for the blood thereof. So, they did not have to be vegetarians anymore. And it was God who made a covenant with Noah.

CHAPTER 3

The Creation

As a point of interest, one galaxy by the name of Sombrero is 28 million light-years away from us and has 800 billion suns! Can you imagine? It would take 28 million years to get there and at the speed of light to boot. How many lifetimes would it take to go 28 million years? At an average life span of 80 years, it would take 350,000 life spans to get there. And we can keep going, 2 galaxies, named hgc 2207 and lc2163 are 114 billion light- years away. This means that we would have to go at the speed of light 114 billion years. That is 183 miles per second and 114 billion years to get there. And the Trifid Nebula is only 9,000 light-years from here. New stars are still being born there. Created? According to NASA, the oldest star in our galaxy, "He 1523-0901" is estimated to have been formed ("created") between 6.5 and 10.1 billion years ago, which is nearly as old as the universe itself *(Wikipedia)*.

I read recently that there are six hundred billion suns in *the Milky Way galaxy* alone, and there are *one hundred billion galaxies* in the observable universe. So again, this makes the Milky Way just an insignificant speck in the universe. It is hard to fathom the immensity of the universe. Yet the Gods decided to create all this out of nothing! And in just one day, or for that matter at the most may be in a thousand years.

But could they? On the fourth day, they created the sun and the moon. However, the moon did not start to orbit earth until ten million years later. Yet, in the creation, it is described as the lesser light to rule the night and was supposed to have been created at the same time as the sun—give or take ten million years?

This is definitely wrong and inaccurate. Now one can say, "How do we know for sure that this is what it is?" In the same line, how can we explain what is in the Bible. And where is the proof that God exists?

In the early 1950s, there was an Irish priest who figured out that the earth was about six thousand years old. He did this by adding up the generations from Adam all the way up to the year zero. One can do that, but it is unlikely to be accurate due because everything came into existence between six and ten billion years ago, not thousands or even millions but *billions* of years ago.

Now we have to notice that religion does realize that they cannot justify this relatively short time frame when there is overwhelming evidence to the contrary in spite of 2 Peter 3:8 "that one day is with the Lord a thousand years." In reality, it would have been more accurate if a day had been similar to ten or even one hundred million years. We know that the sun is also about four and a half billion years old.

One of the Egyptian Gods was Ra, the sun God. The Egyptians knew that if the sun stopped shining, everybody and everything would die. The sun was the giver of all life on earth. That was why they worshipped and saw the sun as a God.

So, in those days, nobody had any idea of or understood the magnitude of the stars and the universe. The Catholic Church—and for that matter, every other church—was of the opinion that the earth was flat and it was the center of the universe. They believed at the time that everything revolved around the earth. And they knew the earth was flat and either square or rectangular, according to Revelation 7:1, which reads, "And after these things I saw four angels standing on the four corners of the earth."

Copernicus, the famous Polish astronomer, got himself in deep water when he proved that the world was round. He actually was condemned and banned from the church, not until recently did the Roman Catholic Church admit that he had been right all along and the Vatican had been wrong. There was a fallacy in the Bible.

The creation continued. In Genesis 1:3, we read that on the first day, God said, "Let there be light," and there was light. And He saw the light was good, and He separated light from darkness. He called the light day, and darkness is the lack of light.

Would He need a whole day to create light and darkness? From all that we know, He needed only a day to create the unimaginable great and big universe. All He said on the first day was "Let there be light," and poof, there it was. What did He do the rest of the day? Plenty of time to rest after a hard day's work.

Genesis 1:14–19 continues the story. It is written in the Bible that on the fourth day, God created two great lights, the sun and the moon. The greater light was to govern the day and to separate light from darkness. It becomes apparent God did what He had already done on the first day, by separating light from darkness.

Now we can see that the creation could have been done in five days instead of six, plus an extra day for rest. Since when do Gods need rest? This shows another human trait. He had to rest? Maybe He likes to take a nap too occasionally? He even mentioned everything was very good! But only at the time of the creation was it "very good."

We know as human beings that after you create or make something, you look back at it and almost all the time you are proud of what you created. Well, so did God.

However, here comes the opposite reaction.

Genesis 6:6–7 says, "And it repented [he was sorry] the Lord that He had made man on the earth and it grieved Him at his heart." But at the time when He supposedly created earth, it was very good. Again, this shows, that God had no idea how the future was going to work out. It also shows in different places in the Bible that He could not foresee what was going to happen.

The following are a couple of examples:

1. Adam did eat from the tree of knowledge. The Lord God did not see coming? No, He did not know that beforehand!
2. He wiped out everything on earth in the flood. And then He felt sorry afterward. Nevertheless, He did wipe out every living thing. Can you picture all those poor animals dying? They had not done anything wrong!
3. When He found out that the Israelites, during the exodus, worshipped a golden calf, He threatened to wipe out all the Israelites. Moses had to talk Him out of it. He did not see that coming either.

It shows, that generally, or most of the time, He did not know what the consequences were going to be from His plans.

Anyhow God duplicated Himself grandiosely, by repeating the first day's actions on the fourth day. Both days He separated the light from the darkness. And then casually it is mentioned that He made the stars also. As far as the writers of the Bible are concerned, those stars were just pretty little lights in the sky. And when they saw a meteor or a comet flying through the sky, then, as far as they were concerned, that was a falling star. This term is still used up to the present time, which makes sense, because that was as far as they could see.

In Revelation 12:4, it says, " … and his tail drew the third part of the stars of heaven, and did cast them to earth." This would mean that trillions and trillions of stars would wipe out the earth and obliterate the planet. Utterly ridiculous! It's an indication that John, the writer of Revelation, had no idea of what stars were, and he was being told by heaven a ridiculous story!

Revelation 8:12 says, "And the fourth angel sounded, and the third part of the sun was smitten and the third part of the moon, and the third part of the stars." How absurd!

Revelation 6:13 states, "And the stars of heaven fell unto the earth." This means almost all those stars must have missed the earth, as billions and billions of stars falling onto the earth would have created a tremendous chaos in the universe. Can you imagine the universe in turmoil?

Billions of stars never could find earth but would fall continuously into space with dire consequences for the universe.

Moses wrote the first five books of the Bible, known as the Pentateuch. Moses was brought up, raised, and taught in the court of the Egyptians and thereby was highly influenced by the Egyptian way of thinking. They had many Gods and they did not believe in the Gods of Israel—probably due to lack of missionaries at that time.

At that time, God did not want to have anything to do with anybody who was not a circumcised Israelite.

The Israelites were still nomads and living in tents at the time, while the Egyptians already had built world wonders, the great pyramids, and they had brick buildings and were living in brick houses.

We, here in the United States, do live mostly in houses that show the consequences after a tornado has hit or when a fire breaks out. Most of the houses in Europe are built with bricks or cement blocks and have the electricity underground or on the roofs instead of by poles delivered to their homes. So, power outages are unheard of during ice storms, fallen trees, and so on. Well, so much for the digressing.

Then He even continued, "And the Lord said: I will destroy man whom I have created from the face of the earth; both man and beast and the creeping thing, and the birds: for it repents me [I am sorry], that I have made them."

How sad for a God to say that! Anyway, had He done what He first said and destroyed man whom He have created, then that would have been the end of the Bible and He would not have had to create his son later either.

Again, He could not foresee that the creation was going to be a fiasco?

In spite of what God said after He finished the creation, "God saw everything He created, and then He said it was "very good." We can see that only for the time being was it very good as far as He could see. Obviously, God had no idea that He was going to be sorry later on for what He had done.

The Second Day of Creation

Now let's see if there is anybody who can make heads or tails out of this one.

Genesis 1:6–8 says, "God said, let there be a firmament in the midst of the waters, and let it divide the waters from the waters. [indicating that the whole earth was originally all water] And now He put land (firmament) in the water] God made the firmament and divided the waters which were under the firmament from the waters which were above the firmament. And God called the firmament heaven."

This sounds like jargon or gobbledygook. No way anybody can picture this situation. How does one divide the waters from under the firmament (heaven) from the waters above the firmament (heaven)? But leave it up to the Christians, they always know and are determined to explain everything.

The third day of creation, everybody becomes a vegetarian.

God said, "Let the earth bring forth grass, the herb yielding seed and the fruit tree yielding fruit," and God saw that it was good again, and the earth brought forth grass and herbs and the tree yielding fruits. So all the herbs and grass were in existence and the fruit trees had fruit on them.

Genesis 1:29 says, "God said I have given you every herb, and every tree: to you it shall be for meat. And it shall be in place of meat."

How did Adam, who was not even created yet, figure out how he had to substitute herbs for meat?

Genesis 1:30 tells us God said, "I have given you every herb." Now how was Adam supposed to know what meat was at this time? There was not a human being or an animal on earth so far. So, was He talking to Himself again? Obviously, because He said, "I have given you every herb." Strange, He was already talking to Adam in spite of him not yet being present. But Gods can do strange things.

"And to every beast of the earth, and to all the fowl, and to everything that creeps on the earth, wherein there is life, I have given every green herb for meat, and it was so." This indicates everybody and every beast and fowl was now a vegetarian.

Again, there were no living creatures around. Thus, He made a degree that everything alive must be a vegetarian. How did He let the animals know that they had to eat herbs?

And God saw that it was very good again. So every living thing became vegetarian. However, He still had to create Adam and all the animals. There is no record that God ever told Adam he had to be a vegetarian, except before he was in existence, but he knew somehow. Maybe through mental telepathy?

What about eagles, vultures, and other birds that live on fish, like pelicans, seagulls, and penguins, to name just a few? So, all animals in the beginning were vegetarians, and later some became carnivores. Penguins, for instance, live on fish, and vegetation is absent. Does this fall into place with the Darwinian theory maybe?

What about crocodiles, alligators, lions, tigers, hyenas, coyotes, and so on? Crocodiles and alligators with their big teeth have to catch animals alive, for example, and they have never been able to eat grass or herbs! It is absurd that God would now expect everybody and each and every animal to be vegetarian. So, from all indications, in the beginning, there were no carnivores, only cows, goats, sheep, deer, boars, oxen, horses, camels, and other grass- and herb-eating animals.

Can you picture crocodiles or pelicans grazing green pastures? They are not exactly built to do that.

Maybe there were only a few basic animals around, like the ones mentioned here. They all ate grass and herbs. Anyway, God expected everybody and every animal to be vegetarian! It is just not possible for every animal to be vegetarian, but if so, then the end result must have come through evolution (Darwin).

Then comes a change. Everybody can eat all kinds of flesh.

In Genesis 9:3, we read that God realizes His mistake and changes everything in midstream. God told Noah after he got out of the ark and made an offer of one of each animal in the ark. And God really did like it; he savored the smell of the meat again. God said, "Every moving thing that lives shall be meat for you"—after wiping out almost all of them on earth—and He continued, "Even as the green herb have I given you all things with one stipulation, and that is, no blood."

"But flesh with the life thereof, which is the blood thereof, shall you not eat."

In Genesis 9:3–5, He tells him, "If you do eat meat with blood in it I will take your life, and I will require it from every beast too." That is strange; how did the animals know about this decree? They eat meat as it is, regardless of the blood, and they like it more, just because of the blood.

Now they all could eat any living thing to their hearts' content. This includes pigs, rabbits, and other (unclean) meat. Now they could eat anything and whatever they desired. Human consumption is obviously not allowed or even mentioned.

In Genesis 9:3–4, Noah and his family were supposedly the only ones on earth. It was just after the flood when God was telling this to Noah. Just like Adam and his woman, Noah and his family were the only ones around!

A new edict came about—what to eat and what not to eat.

In Leviticus 11:2–8, we read that it was in the time of Moses that God himself gave instructions to Moses and Aaron, who were to tell the Israelites not to eat the meat from camels, hares, coneys (which are rabbits), and also pigs. Strictly forbidden! This includes the side products, like ham and bacon from pigs. All of the above-mentioned animals are unclean!

God continues, "These you shall eat of all that are in the waters: whatsoever has fins and scales, in the waters, and in seas, and in rivers. And all that have no fins or scales, of any living thing in the waters shall be an abomination to you."

This means you definitely were not allowed to eat crabs or crab legs or shrimp, lobster, lobster tails, eels, oysters, clams or abalones, or whales, just to name a few again.

God continues, "You shall not eat certain birds: the eagle, the ossifrage, (a sea eagle), and the osprey (a hawk), and the vulture, and the owl, the night hawk, the cuckoo, and the swan, and the pelican, and the stork, and the bat and some more birds," which makes sense, "and you shall not eat fowls that creep, going on all four, they shall be an abomination to you" (Leviticus 11:20).

Must be an extinct bird that can creep on all fours and fly? Maybe He is talking about Pegasus, the winged horse, or dragons or flying dinosaurs.

Observe, please, that after Leviticus 11:2 through 8, which tells us which animals could be eaten and which ones could not, in Deuteronomy 12:15, Now Moses gives the command, "Notwithstanding, you may kill and eat flesh in all thy gates, whatsoever your soul lusts after, according to the blessing of the Lord thy God, which he has given thee, the unclean and the clean may eat thereof, as of the roebuck and the hart. Only ye shall not eat the blood." So now they can eat everything their heart desires again—a complete 180-degree turn.

In Deuteronomy 12:23, Moses is still talking, and he says it again: "As I commanded thee, and thou shall eat in thy gates whatsoever thy soul lusted after. Even as the roebuck and the hart are eaten, so thou shall eat them: the unclean and the clean shall eat of them alike."

In Acts 10:15 and Acts 11, for the fifth time, there is a change again. God shows Peter all the unclean animals and declares them all clean. In a vision, he tells him to kill and eat. Peter says, "Not me, Lord, for I have never eaten anything that is unclean." Peter knew it was the Lord speaking.

Then the voice of God said, "What God has cleaned, you shall not call unclean."

God told Peter to eat unclean meat. And now anyone, except Jews and Muslims, can eat pigs, rabbits, and other unclean animals to their hearts' content!

In Revelation 18:2, the unclean is mentioned again: "Babylon the great has fallen and it becomes the habitat of devils and a cage of every unclean and hateful bird." In the New Testament, God told Peter, that from then on, there were no more unclean animals. However, at the end of the world, they show up again.

God shows that vacillation on five occasions:

1) He starts from vegetarianism (Genesis 1:29).
2) People can eat anything they want to eat as long as it has no blood in it (Genesis 3:3–4).
3) The people receive a list of what to eat, what is clean, and what not to eat because it is unclean (Leviticus 11:2,8).
4) He goes back to allowing them to eat anything they want to eat again but no blood (Deuteronomy 12:15).
5) Then they go back to being able to eat each and everything, including blood this time (Acts 10:15).

Wishy-washy again to say the least. Is this a God who cannot make up His mind? Can He not make a decision on what is the right thing and good for people to eat anytime? So, God is not good at decision making, and He can't look into the future!

God made the stars. Genesis 1:16 describes how God made two great lights, the sun and the moon, and He made the stars also.

God set them in the "firmament of the heaven" to give light upon the earth. Stars, besides the sun, don't give any light here on earth; they are visible all right, but if there is no moon, then with a clear sky, it will still be pitch-dark.

Now, first, what is the firmament of the heaven? Is it the heaven of the heaven? Earlier in the creation, He called the firmament heaven (Genesis 1:8). Confusing.

All this shows is that the writers of the creation did not have any idea of what the stars were besides pretty little lights in the sky. We can't blame them, because that was all they could see and knew at that time. And they got the wrong inspiration from God? They did not have any idea yet of galaxies, nebulae, and the infinite universe.

God saw everything He had made, and it was very good. Six times, it says, "And it was good." He could not foresee what was going to happen, the omniscient (all-knowing) and omnipotent (all powerful) God did not know what the future had in store!

It was only temporarily good or very good, as we will see.

Genesis 2:5 tells us nothing was growing because the Lord had not caused it to rain. How inconsistent! First, He brought forth all the grass, herbs, and trees, and He made everything alive eat herbs. And He, God, saw it was good.

Then, after the seventh day, after the creation, the Lord noticed that it had not rained, so nothing had grown supposedly.

Genesis 2:5 says, "And every plant of the field before it was in the earth, and every herb before it grew." So, everything was growing. Now as a contradiction, the verse continues, "for the Lord God had not caused it to rain."

In spite of no rain, everything was growing. This is what it literally says word for word: "And every herb of the field before it grew for the lord had not caused it to rain." God works in mysterious ways, does He not? A glaring contradiction or an error made by the writers of the Bible?

This indicates that whoever wrote the Bible had not figured it out correctly, in spite of everybody being told by religion that the Bible is written by inspiration from God. And the Bible is supposed to be God's word!

Again, the writers wrote the Bible in the relatively short time period after creation and obviously had no idea that the stars were just as big as earth and even many times larger than earth. To them, they appeared to be just pretty lights in the sky at night. This includes God.

In the book of Revelation, it is mentioned a few times that the stars fell on the earth; this is at the end of the world. This is preposterous! One star by its self would completely obliterate the earth. But if you look at stars as little lights, then those little lights can fall on the earth without destroying it. Not to mention, *all* the stars would supposedly fall on the earth. This is absolutely absurd as there are billions and billions of them!

In comparison, if God had created all the stars, planets, and constellations, as mentioned in the Bible, at the speed of light, then He probably needed less than a nanosecond to make the earth! Creating the earth is peanuts compared to creating the universe! The earth is just an insignificant part of the universe. Besides God could never have finished the universe, because it is infinite and is still growing and losing stars.

CHAPTER 4

The Creation of Man

Genesis 1:26–28 reads, "And God said: let us create man in our image, after our likeness. So, God created man in his own image, in the image of God created He him. [Observe, he created "man" in his image, not male and female in his image. It seems the "male and female created He them" was added later.] And God blessed them, and told them, be fruitful and multiply."

How can one man be fruitful and multiply? "Let us create man in our image. In the image of God created He him." The "him" was created both male and female. He had not yet created the female, known as "Eve" or Adam's woman. She was later made from a rib from Adam, and she became his "helpmeet."

If God had created the female right there, then there would have been two of them in the Garden of Eden. No, God said, "Let us make man in our image."

Originally, from what we can deduct, it becomes clear the Lord's plan was to have one man only in the Garden of Eden. And He made the man, and He made him male and female. This is known as a hermaphrodite. The dictionary defines *hermaphrodite* as an individual with both male and female reproductive organs. We can make the conclusion that if Adam was made in God's image, then the Gods must be hermaphrodites too. There is nothing wrong with being a hermaphrodite though.

Occasionally, babies are still being born with both sexes. The medical profession does not make a big deal out of it. They must be throwbacks to the time of Adam. They just make the baby one sex or leave it for later, when it is decided what is best for the child to become, a boy or a girl.

Male bodies, up to the present time, still have breasts, some as big as women's, but most are flat chested. Big male breasts are mostly due, it is claimed, to the use of marijuana. Nevertheless, every man still has nipples, showing that originally, they must have had actual breasts also.

Genesis 2:4 gives the generations of heaven and of earth. This, in essence, is a synopsis or a summary of what happened earlier. Again, it is contradictory, to say the least.

Genesis 2:7 says, "And the Lord formed Man out of the dust of the ground." This time, God did not create, but the Lord did. Adam was already created in God's image on the sixth day and now He made him again, this time out of dust and not in his image.

In Genesis 2:19, to top it off, "out of the ground, the Lord God formed every beast of the field and every fowl of the air; and brought them to Adam to see what he would call them." Because He did not know? Here we go again! We would expect the Lord to know everything beforehand.

The Lord is curious? He wanted to see what Adam would call them. Notice that the Lord definitely did not know what Adam would call those animals. This indicates the Lord does not know our thoughts either.

All those birds flying in formation in front of Adam or waddling in front of him and the many other species of animals in the parade, he had to name. How could Adam have the vocabulary to name all those animals? He had not spoken a word yet to anybody. The all-knowing/omniscient God did not know what Adam was going to call the animals. God is curious? This can be attributed to what human beings are. He is expected to know everything. The all-knowing/omniscient God did not know that beforehand either?

Maybe Adam did call them "duh," "duh-duh," "dah," "duh-dah," and so on? Or whatever.

It makes one wonder if he saw any dinosaurs. And could he have named a polar bear? Polar bears, for one, could not have existed in the environment of Asia Minor for all that long, so they never were in the animal parade. Neither were there any penguins and so on.

How about chimpanzees, orangutans, and gorillas? Did Adam name all the types of dinosaurs, in spite of dinosaurs already being extinct at that time, and even before God could have created them and other extinct animals, like the woolly mammoth or saber-toothed tiger. He would have to have given several hundreds of names. Put yourself in Adam's place and see if you could come up with over a hundred names.

Genesis 2:5 tells us that after the creation of Adam by the Lord Himself, the Lord claims, "And there was not a man to till the ground." So, man was made just so he could till the ground? Adam was made to work the ground. It seems that must have been an important reason for the Lord to make a person. So, he could plant what?

How could anybody, after he just came into existence, till the ground anyhow? With his bare hands? There were no shovels or other gadgets yet.

When Adam was kicked out of the Garden of Eden, the Lord "cursed is the ground for your sake" (Genesis 3:17). And when Noah came out of the ark, the Lord said, "I will not again curse the ground, anymore for man's sake." We can see that "the ground" was very important for the Gods.

Adam had no experience in what had to be done unless he was created a master gardener, but that is not likely. We can deduce from this that the purpose for Adam in life was to be a farmer. After Adam was kicked out of the Garden of Eden, then God cursed the ground for Adam's sake. Now he had to work. "And in the sweat of your face shall you eat bread" (Genesis 3:19)—not make bread but eat it.

At least Adam and his woman knew how to make bread then. They knew how to bake bread? This indicates that they must have known how to make fire also. That is remarkable! Besides, how much sweating is there if you only have to make bread for two people?

In Genesis 2:19, we learn the Lord does not know what Adam is going to call all the animals. He wanted to see what Adam would call them; that is what He said. So how can he know what we are planning or thinking or doing?

He formed Adam out of the dust of the ground. And we know, not in God's image this time. We only know that after He made Adam, He blew in his nostrils the breath of life and He became a living soul. Adam was alive!

Now we have to digress a little bit. When a baby is born, then the doctor makes the baby cry, and when it starts crying, it takes in a breath of air; now the baby becomes a living soul. Now and only now, the baby is alive, after taking the first breath.

The baby, while still in the womb and before it takes its first breath, begins to show signs of life after a certain amount of time. Its heart starts beating, and it moves about—all this by means of the umbilical cord, which keeps the baby growing until birth. In the meantime, the heart grows, and the other organs do too. The fetus moves, for if it did not, it could not grow bigger. So, it has to be that way. If one would take the umbilical cord away from the fetus when in the womb, then the baby would die right away.

Quite a few more places in the Bible it is brought up "anything that has in it the breath of life" is alive. But, in essence, what is missing is always the first breath—*the breath of life.*

This means that after being born, it becomes a living soul but only after taking the first breath, just like Adam became a living soul after the Lord God breathed into his nostrils the breath of life. In other words, if there is an abortion, then the beginning of life is killed, but not a living human or a baby, which becomes a living soul only when the baby is out of the womb and after taking its first breath of air. The Bible has nothing to do with the "life starts at conception" idea, even if it appears to be alive.

It is mentioned again in Genesis 6:17, "Behold I do bring a flood of waters on the earth, to destroy all flesh, wherein is the breath of life." In other words, if there is no breath of life, then life does not exist.

Genesis 2:8 says, "And the Lord God planted a garden eastward in Eden." This indicates there was already a city or maybe a territory existing by the name of Eden. Otherwise, "the Lord planted a garden," would have been sufficient. So, God made a garden eastward in a territory or city called Eden.

There he put the man he had formed, and not the one that was created in God's image. So, the man who was created in God's image is now out of the picture. It is only the man whom God had formed out of the dust; he is the one everybody supposedly up to this day is derived from. He put the tree of life and the tree of knowledge in the middle of the garden (of Eden). And the Lord God took the man (Adam)—still no woman—and put him in the Garden of Eden to dress it and to keep it. There were not supposed to be any weeds.

Adam had no experience in what he had to do. Maybe he had to pick up dead branches and leaves? No, he was made to till the ground.

After Adam was kicked out the Garden of Eden, God cursed the ground for Adam's sake. Now he had to work.

"And in the sweat of your face shall you eat bread"—not make bread, but eat it.

In Genesis 3:19, God instructs Adam not to eat from the tree of knowledge.

"And the Lord God commanded the man, saying, of every tree you can freely eat, but not from the tree of knowledge of good and evil. For in the day you eat thereof you shall surely die."

Ironically, next to the tree of knowledge was the tree of life, right smack in the middle of the Garden of Eden, side by side (Genesis 2:9).

Adam had no idea of what dying was all about, so it probably did not make all that much of an impression on him when he was told "You will die the same day if you eat from that tree."

Back to the creation. Adam got a woman.

There was no helpmeet for Adam. That's all God called it, a helpmeet and not a wife.

Genesis 2:21 says, "And the Lord God caused a deep sleep to fall on Adam, and He took one of his ribs and made a woman out of it. And Adam said: she shall be called woman, because she was taken out of man. [We know now it is possible that God somehow cloned the woman from the female side of Adam. How did Adam know he was missing a rib and that the woman was made from his rib?] And they were both naked, and they were not ashamed." In front of whom would they be ashamed and of what? Each other?

They did not think anything about it, because that was how it was! They obviously had no idea what sex was either!

Back to the creation again.

As a matter of fact, everything He made was so good that he had to destroy all the plants, trees, and animals, even humans, in the still-to-come flood. The all-knowing, omniscient God could not foresee that He would have to make a decision to wipe out everything He created again!

Genesis 6: 6–7 says, "And the Lord said: I will destroy man whom I have created from the face of the earth, both man, and beast and fowls. I have made them." Why the beasts and the fowls also? They did not do anything wrong. This does not sound like much of a Lord, because He cannot foresee the consequences of what He is planning on doing, like wiping out all of the humans and the animals and birds. The beasts and the fowls did not do anything to offend the Lord; they were just innocent animals. How could the Lord be sorry? He, God, made the animals Himself. He talked without or contrary to reason. It shows throughout the Bible the Lord does not care much about animals, unless they are offered to Him on an altar and when He can smell the meat and savor it.

Nevertheless, it looks like He wanted to have a clean slate, by threatening to wipe each and every living thing from the face of the earth. But we know He could not do that, because this would mean He would have to do the creation all over again. Fortunately, He found Noah. So, we are saved because of Noah.

He created the animals and the fowl. It also seems that humans can't exist without animals. That is why God had Noah put two of each in the ark, so they could procreate.

First, He made everything so it was very good, and then He regretted that He had done it. Somehow, He could not foresee the future. This is sad for an all- knowing, omnipotent God. Obviously, He did not think too much of the creation. This was His handiwork and supposedly his masterpiece.

Genesis 6:6 says, "And it repented the Lord that He had made man on earth, and it grieved him at his heart."

We can deduce that the stay in the Garden of Eden for Adam and his wife did not last all that long. Because there is not much data recorded about the relatively short time Adam was in the Garden of Eden.

CHAPTER 5

The Fall of Adam and His Woman

The Garden of Eden is also known by many people as paradise. Paradise is mentioned twice and only in the New Testament!

When Jesus hung on the cross, He said to the one hanging next to Him, "Today you will be with me in paradise" (Luke 23:43). This would have been nice for the guy; however, Jesus did not go to "paradise" that day but many days later.

Revelation 2:7 says, "To him that overcomes will I give to eat of the tree of life, which is in the midst of the paradise of God." However, when in heaven, one is not supposed to be in need of the tree of life. You are supposed to already have eternal life. This is something new, because souls are not supposed to eat either.

Anyhow, nowhere is paradise synonymous with the Garden of Eden, just in folklore. You hear people saying this place is like paradise, when something looks and feels fantastic, more or less like an Elysium.

The female known by the name Eve was never in the Garden of Eden. At least not by that name.

After they were kicked out of the Garden of Eden, Adam called his wife Eve, because he said she was the mother of all living (Genesis 3:20). Now she could get children, and that was why Adam called her Eve?

While in the Garden of Eden, she was known as his woman, "And Adam said: she shall be called woman," after she was created from one of his ribs.

Genesis 2:25 says, "And they were both naked, the man and his wife, and they were not ashamed." Why would they be ashamed and of what? Each other? They were supposedly the only ones around.

How could that happen? They never observed that they were different. They were from the beginning naked and obviously did not think much about it.

That was how they were when they saw each other for the first time, and they must have looked upon it as being natural.

This indicates sex did not happen in the Garden of Eden, because only after they were out of the Garden of Eden did they have sex. Then they did have children, and that's why Adam called her the mother of all living. Then they knew what sex was and that she could have children.

Sex is a downfall for a lot of people. We only have to look at priests and even bishops having sex with girls or little boys. And in other Christian churches, ministers and preachers have done the same. A lot of husbands and wives are not faithful with each other too.

Survival comes first for humankind. A human being will do anything to survive. Animals will do the same thing (Ron Hubbard). Second is sex! That is family and kids (Ron Hubbard). Even in the military, they teach this. There is nothing wrong with sex—except when done in criminal situations, like rape.

Genesis 3:15 says, "The serpent was more subtle than any beast of the field which the lord God had made." Yes, God created this animal that could talk and reason. He made the serpent subtle, which is crafty, skillful, ingenious, clever, and refined, according to the *Funk and Wagnalls Dictionary* definition of *subtle*. So, it was

God's prerogative to make that subtle animal, and He did just that! Even Jesus said, "Be ye therefore wise as serpents" (Matthew 10:16).

"And the serpent said to the woman: yea, has God said you shall not eat of every tree in the garden? And she said to the serpent, we may eat of every tree in the garden, but not from the tree in the middle of the garden, God has said, you shall not eat of it, neither shall you touch it, lest you die" (Genesis 3:1–3).

Did God hang a sign on the tree that said, "Do not eat from this tree or you'll die"? No, they were told.

Only two trees were in the middle of the garden, the tree of life and the tree of knowledge of good and evil (Genesis 2:9). So, one tree was good and the other one was bad, and both trees were right in the middle of the garden.

"And the serpent said: you shall not surely die, for God knows that in the day you eat thereof your eyes shall be opened, and you shall be as Gods, knowing good and evil" (Genesis 3:4–5). So the serpent did not lie to the woman.

Genesis 3:22 states, "And the Lord God said, behold the man is become like one of us, to know good and evil." This indicates that Adam and his woman, while living in the garden, had no idea of what evil was. But they became "like one of us," which means like Gods. Humans became like Gods at this time and knew good and evil but they were mortals.

Now Adam was there all the time, when the dialogue was going on between the woman and the serpent. Not a peep out of him. He also could not see anything wrong with the reasoning of the serpent, so it seems.

So, "When the woman saw that the tree was good for food, and attractive to the eyes, and a tree to be desired, to make one wise, than she plucked the fruit…" (Genesis 3:6). One cannot blame them, for they were not wise yet! How can one know that a tree will make you wise? They were not told.

"She took the fruit from the tree, and did eat, and she gave also to Adam, and he ate" (Genesis 3:6). Did Adam get smart, and did he get inspiration from God? No, because God was not even aware of what was going on!

Did Adam say, "Oh no, honey, don't do that. We are not allowed to do that," or whatever he could have said? No, sir. He took the fruit also. "She handed him and he touched it also and he ate" (Genesis 3:6).

"And the eyes of both of them were opened" (Genesis 3:7). In other words, they looked at each other and could see they were naked because their eyes were opened.

All the time they were in the garden before they ate from the forbidden tree, they never noticed they were naked, but they were naked all the time nevertheless. This is what the serpent said to the woman: "Your eyes will be opened." They had no idea what would happen when their eyes were opened.

"And they heard the voice of the Lord God walking in the garden in the cool of the day" (Genesis 3:8). In the Bibles in Europe, except England, it says, "And they were walking in the coolness of the evening breeze," which makes more sense than walking in the cool of the day. This, in essence, could also be in the evening.

As mentioned earlier, God obviously was not talking to Himself or singing when they heard the voice of God. Well, they hid themselves among the trees. Apparently, God was used to having Adam and his woman coming to him when He came into the garden, just like a doggy does when he sees his master walking in the garden. This time, however, no Adam. So, God did not see Adam. He had to call Adam, "Where are you?" And Adam said, "I heard your voice, I heard you talking, in the garden, and I was afraid, because I was naked" (Genesis 3:9–10).

Again, this is a classic example of God not being aware of what was going on! He had to ask, "Where were you?" He was not aware of what had happened.

"Then God said: who told you that you were naked?" (Genesis 3:11). He had to ask again. Nobody had told Adam that he was naked, so he could not answer that question. But the Lord had

56

to ask anyhow. Again, this is another indication of God being in the dark and not knowing what was going on.

God starts to interrogate Adam and his woman. The Gods went down to the Garden of Eden when it was getting cool down there, and it must have been a pleasure to walk in the garden. The Gods did not have any idea of what had happened earlier, so they just went down to enjoy themselves in the garden.

Most likely it was the day after Adam and his woman took of the forbidden tree. They looked at each other and saw that they were naked. Their eyes were opened. Now they wanted each other, and nobody had to show them how to make love. Nature probably took its course.

Sometime later, they decided to sew fig leaves together to make aprons out of those leaves. This would have taken some time, because they certainly did not have any experience making aprons, and they had to do it using trial and error. And they were probably nervous to boot. In the meantime, the Gods were going down to the Garden of Eden, unaware of what had happened.

First, He had to call for Adam, "Where are you?" when Adam did not show up to greet Him. If He could not find two people in a garden, then it should be impossible to find any of us among billions of people. Now there are more than six billion people here on earth!

"And Adam said, I heard your voice in the garden, and I was afraid, because I was naked, and I hid myself" (Genesis 3:10).

God started to ask questions one after another. First, He asked, "Who told you that you were naked?" This question could not be answered. Nobody had told Adam or his woman that they were going to notice their nakedness in spite of them having been naked all the time. Then He asked, "Have you eaten from the tree of which I commanded you not to eat?" He was getting suspicious.

It would have made more sense if God said, "You have eaten from the tree of which I had commanded you not to eat from, and this will be your punishment."

No, sir. He wanted to find out what had happened and get to the bottom of it by asking questions. Because He did not know!

Now did Adam say, "Yes, I did and I am very sorry. Please forgive me"? No, Adam attempted to put the blame on God Himself and on his woman. Adam said, "The woman you gave to me, she gave me of the tree" (Genesis 3:12). In other words, "I did not ask for her. You gave her to me, and she gave me the fruit to eat." What a cop-out that was! But God did not bite.

Adam, in essence, said, "I did not ask for her; you gave her to me." He did not want to admit he was also liable and responsible for his deed. Nevertheless, God saw by Adam's statement that she had had something to do with it too. So, He said to the woman, "What is this that you have done?" Again, God did not know! And she tried to do the same thing Adam did, but she blamed the serpent. "So, she said, the serpent beguiled me, and I did eat" (Genesis 3:13). God got the idea and started with the serpent, the one He had made Himself. So, God ignored her answer too.

The punishments for Adam, his woman, the serpent, and Satan, if he was also involved, was not all that severe.

God made the serpent, as mentioned earlier. The Gods might have said, "Let's use the serpent and tempt Adam and his woman and see if they do what we have told them not to." God likes to tempt.

He did it also with Abraham. He was to offer his only son to God. Fortunately, God stopped him just in time. Can you imagine Abraham coming back home, Sarah asking him, "Where is Isaac?" and then Abraham telling her, "I offered him up to God"? That would have been, in all probability, the end of Abraham too.

Jesus, in teaching us how to pray, said, "Lead us not into temptation." Even Jesus knew that God would tempt if He thought it was a good idea for him to tempt!

Deuteronomy 4:34 says, "Or has God assayed to go and take him a nation from the midst of another nation, by temptations, by signs, and by wonders, and by war, according to all that the Lord your God did for you in Egypt before your eyes"? This applies to

Israel taken out of Egypt. Here, the Lord admits that He used temptations to get the Israelites out of Egypt.

God could not have said, "Let's use the serpent and Satan," because God has no control over Satan.

God started addressing the serpent and not by saying, "What have you done?" No. The serpent did not have a chance to answer God and say if he did it or if it was Satan who did it. No, God starts directly cursing the serpent, "Because you have done this you are cursed above all cattle, and over every beast in the field, on your belly shall you go and dust you shall eat all of your life" (Genesis 3:14). Maybe God felt a kind of foolish that He did not know right away what the situation was.

This was the first time God cursed but not the last.

It is commonly assumed that the serpent is synonymous with Satan, because this makes everything that went wrong easy to explain. When God created the animal known as the serpent, He definitely did not create Satan. Satan was already in existence and at present is still residing in heaven with his angels. Yes, the devil has angels too, just like God has angels (See Revelation 12:7–8). However, in Revelation 12:15–17, the serpent is synonymous with a dragon (This all is supposed to be at the time when the world is nearing its end):

"And there was war in heaven: Michael and his angels fought the dragon and his angels, and prevailed not, neither was there place found any more in heaven." It says here Michael did not prevail! A problem of sentence structure?

"And the great dragon was cast out on the earth" (Revelation 12:9). And the great dragon was not called a "serpent"!

So, as of right now, Satan is still free to go wherever he wants to in heaven until the end of the world! And chances are you might still meet him there when you go to heaven. That's only if you go to heaven.

That poor animal that God created gets the brunt of the punishment. He is the one who gets cursed.

The other possibility is that Satan entered the serpent. But why would he do that? Adam and his woman had never heard of Satan. And God did not warn Adam and his woman about possible impending disasters; again, they could not foresee what was going to happen. The only thing Adam was told was not to eat from that tree or "the day you eat there of you shall surely die" (Genesis 2:17). But they did not die. And God never told them to watch out for Satan or that there even was a Satan!

So, God had no idea that Satan was going to screw up the works. The amazing thing is, if God had never put that tree in the garden, then nothing could have gone wrong. But then there would not have been a temptation for Adam. Nevertheless, if it was Satan, he messed up God's plan.

In this case, that poor serpent, which God had created Himself (Genesis 3:1) was the one who got cursed and got the worst punishment of everybody involved. God did not punish Satan at all. Why the serpent? All because God had no control over Satan!

God said to the serpent, "Because you have done this you are cursed" (Genesis 3:14). God had said to Adam and his woman, "The day you eat there of you will surely die." That was not true either.

The woman lived a long time after the fall. How old she was when she died is not known. No women's ages at time of death are shown in the Bible, except for Sarah's (Genesis 23:1).

Adam lived to a ripe age of 930 years.

One should realize, had they died after eating the forbidden fruit, which God did warn them about, then that would have been the end of the creation! Again, God did not see the whole situation as it would unravel. He had said, "In the day you eat from that tree, you will die." But they did not die. This could never happen. The Gods would have had to start the creation over again as far as human beings were concerned. But God could not foresee that.

Maybe the earth and animals would have survived this time.

Now to come back to the serpent, we will see that God generally does not care much about animals, even the ones He personally created, except later when animals are offered to Him on an altar, because He savors the smell of burned meat. And, boy oh boy, all through the Old Testament, He commands most of the offers to be burned meat, so He can savor the smell.

And the serpent's curse? "And I will put enmity between thee and the woman. [*Enmity*, according to the dictionary, is a deep-seated unfriendliness or hostility. We know how most women have an inherited fear of snakes.] And between your seed and her seed. [This means enmity between your (the serpent's) seed and her seed.] It shall bruise your head [*Bruise* means to injure, as by a blow, without breaking the surface of the skin, discoloring it. Not much damage done, just discoloring of the skin, like a black eye.] (Genesis 3:15).

"It [the enmity] shall bruise thy head [the serpent's head], and thou [the serpent] shall bruise his heel." A blue spot on his heel?

Whose heel is God talking about? Adam's heel by chance? All in all, not much damage done, just blue spots. Not much straight talk going on here either. In Greek mythology, there is talk about Achilles' heel. Did the writer of Genesis pick up on this maybe?

The punishment given to the woman? "To the woman He said I will greatly multiply thy sorrow and your conception; in sorrow shall you bring forth children" [The saying now is life starts at conception.] And your desire shall be to your husband. And he shall rule over you. [With this text, some religions do keep their wives under control. You better do it because it says so in the Bible!]" (Genesis 3:16).

This part of conception did not make much of an impression on the woman, so how could she know what sorrow was during conception? Conception comes about through sex. So where comes sorrow from conception?

God said, "I will greatly multiply your pain during child birth." If you don't know what pain is, then so what? Later she found out, but at the time, pain at child birth did not mean anything to her.

To Adam, He said, "Because you listened to your wife, and you ate from the tree I commanded you not to eat of, cursed is the ground for your sake" (Genesis 3:17). Here He goes again, not very becoming for a God to curse. This is, so far, the second time that He cursed.

Remember: before the Lord created Adam, he said, "And there was not a man to till the ground." So that's why he cursed the ground. The ground must be very important to God. "Cursed is the ground for your sake."

Anyway, this does not mean that we should not listen to our wives. Quite often, they can come up with magnificent ideas (Genesis 3:18).

"And you shall eat the herb of the field." However, God earlier had already ordered them to eat the herb of the field (Genesis 1:30). So that was not much of a punishment. Just continue what you are doing.

Genesis 3:19 says, "And in the sweat of your face shall you eat bread. In the sweat of thy face shall you eat bread till you return into the ground: For out of it you were taken: for dust you are, and to dust you shall return." Because in Genesis 2:7, God formed the man out of the dust of the ground. And that worked. He had to make man out of dust, and it is never mentioned it was in His image this time! It would be interesting to see what type of DNA Adam had, Maybe, he had no DNA. But the human race slowly evolved into the DNA we have now.

It sounds like Adam was the one who got the curse and not humankind. For Adam was the only one made out of dust. Humankind was and is not made out of dust; they are made out of sperm and eggs, which we can hardly call dust. Or are they?

"And the Lord God made coats out of skins." The first fur coats ever made. Did He kill an animal, or did He take them from animals that died?

Expulsion from the Garden

Genesis 3:5 says, "The serpent said, for God knows, that in the day you eat thereof, your eyes shall be opened, and you shall be as Gods, knowing good and evil."

The Lord continued, "And now, lest he takes also of the tree of life, and eat, he will live forever."

This proves contrary to religion that Adam and his woman did not have eternal life while living in the Garden of Eden.

Adam and his woman could have high-tailed it to the tree of life, but it did not occur to them and they did not because they had no idea what the tree of life could do for them and they were never told by God either.

So, Adam did not have eternal life before the fall, as some people claim.

I was told when I was a little kid that Adam would have lived forever if he hadn't taken fruit from the forbidden tree. But that was not true.

Now they were like Gods, but they had been and still were mortals.

What was the purpose of creation? God made Adam and his woman, they did not have eternal life, and they did not know sex. So, they could not get any offspring. Otherwise, they would have outgrown the Garden of Eden. No, the Gods wanted only one person. Later they changed their minds and made two people, so they could observe them like we do animals in a zoo or an aquarium.

We now know the purpose of creation. It is "And for your pleasure they are and were created" (Revelation 4:11).

But why did God never tell Adam that if he ate from the tree of life he could live forever? He let that go, so that just by chance, they could have tried that fruit, but they never did, obviously. "Now the Lord God drove out the man out of the Garden of Eden, and He placed at the east of the garden of Eden Cherubims, to keep the way of the tree of life." Again, at the east! The Garden of Eden was eastward in Eden (Genesis 2:8). And He placed at the east of the garden of Eden Cherubim (Genesis 3:24). "And Cain dwelt in the land of Nod, on the east of Eden" (Genesis 4:16).

Observe, it does not say on the east of the Garden of Eden, but again on the east of Eden, indicating Eden must have been an important place. This was already in existence before the creation. So, it makes one wonder if there ever was a creation?

What a waste of manpower those cherubim! God could have just destroyed that tree or let it die, so that the magic powers of that tree would have no effect on anybody anymore. And for how long did that tree exist?

There is a reference to a tree of life in Revelation (22:2). Did He transplant it to heaven? Not likely, but read on.

"In heaven and in the midst of the street of it, and on either side of the river, was there the tree of life, which bare twelve types of fruits; every month." This indicates there was more than one tree, "in the middle of the street, and on either side of the river"—so at least three trees of life.

Strange and weird it is that they have streets in heaven. For bicycles and horse-drawn wagons maybe?

But who needs the tree of life in heaven? Once there, you are supposed to have eternal life. Maybe for a snack or some kind of booster?

By then, there should have been millions and millions of "saved souls" in heaven. Three trees would not do much for all those souls. Besides souls are not likely to need any food because physical bodies just decompose here on earth and thus don't go to heaven. Don't ever think your body goes to heaven! If anything goes, it is the soul. And souls don't eat, so the fruit mentioned earlier is probably just nice to look at or for decoration.

Now we are going to look at a hypothetical situation. What would have happened when God came looking for Adam, if they had acted like nothing had happened? Then God would not have known that they had eaten from the tree. But alas that was not what happened. They gave themselves away by hiding and saying, "I am naked." Then God knew something was amiss.

CHAPTER 6

The Story of Cain and Abel

Once there was a mother who had two sons. The oldest son was doing something in the garage. The youngest son went into the garage and asked his older brother, "What are you doing?"

The older brother told him, "I am making a present for Mother." The younger brother said, "That's nice. I am going to do that too."

So, the boys went to their mother with their presents, and would you believe it, she said, "Thank you," to the youngest son. "I like your present very much." Then she said to the oldest boy, "I don't like your present."

Now what mother would do and say such a thing? In reality, there would not be any mother who would treat her kids like that.

Now for the real story:

After Adam and his wife were kicked out of the Garden of Eden, Adam knew his wife, and she got a boy named Cain. Adam knew her again, and she had a second son, Cain's younger brother, Abel. And Abel became a keeper of sheep, but Cain was a tiller of the ground, like Adam was supposed to be, so he was a farmer, and the Lord had cursed the ground for Adam's sake.

Now, in Genesis 4:3–4, Cain offered his produce to the Lord. Nobody told him or forced him to do that, so it was Cain's idea.

He was the first one who came up with the idea of making an offering. Even Adam had never done this.

Genesis 4:3–5 says, "And it came to pass, that Cain brought of the fruit of the ground an offering to the Lord. And Abel brought of the firstlings of his flock and the fat thereof. And the Lord had respect for Abel and his offering. But to Cain and his offering He had no respect."

So Abel copied Cain in making an offering. This was nice of him too—not the copying but the offering. Nevertheless, he did what Cain did. This means if it had not been for Cain making an offering, Abel would not have done so either.

Obviously, as already mentioned earlier, the Lord liked the smell of meat better than the produce. How does produce, fruit of the ground, smell when you offer it? All through the Bible, the statement is made over and over, when an offering of meat is being made to the Lord that the Lord smelled a sweet savor. Examples follow:

Genesis 8:21 says, "And the Lord smelled a sweet savor" (odor).

Exodus 29:18 says, "And you shall burn the whole ram on the altar. It is a burned offering to the Lord; it is a sweet savor, an offering made by fire to the Lord. For a sweet savor before the Lord."

Leviticus 1:13, 17, and 19; Leviticus 2:2, 9, and 12; and Numbers 15:3 make similar references among many more occasions—"Of a sweet savour unto the Lord."

Hebrews 11:4 says, "By faith, Abel offered to the Lord a more excellent sacrifice than Cain."

A more excellent sacrifice? Because it smelled better than the produce? Because Cain's offer did not smell as nice as meat? So, He liked meat better than produce. This indicates God is prejudiced in this case.

"And Cain was very wroth [filled with anger and incensed] and his countenance fell [*countenance* is facial expression]." Would you not be ticked off if you came up with the original idea of bringing an offering to God—nobody had done this before, not even Adam—and then your little brother copied your idea and got the grand prize?

"And the Lord said to Cain: why are you angry, and why is your facial expression off?"

The Lord had to ask questions again, like He did not know that Cain was the first one who came up with the idea to bring, voluntarily, an offer to the Lord.

Cain did not feel like defending himself. He was the originator of the idea of bringing an offering to the Lord, and he wanted to please the Lord. Even Adam had never done that before. He was a volunteer, but the Lord did not like his offering. Why not? Because when God smelled the offering from Abel, a lamb, it must have smelled a heck of a lot better than Cain's produce did. The Lord shows he is biased; he likes meat better than produce.

"And Cain talked with Abel, when they were in the field, and Cain slew Abel." They got into an argument, and Abel must have said the wrong thing to Cain, who was already on edge, something that really ticked him off. Cain hit Abel, and Abel died.

This was the first death ever, so most likely, Cain did not know that he could kill Abel when he hit him. He did not know what death was and that if he hit him at the wrong place, then death could occur. So Cain must have hit Abel on the wrong spot or Abel might have brought the episode up again, which probably put Cain in a rage so he hit him with disastrous results.

"And the Lord said to Cain where is your brother?" Again, He had to ask, because He supposedly heard the blood of Abel crying from the ground.

The Lord asked, "Do you happen to know where Abel, your brother, is?" And Cain came back with a wisecrack. "Am I my brother's keeper?"

That ticked the Lord off probably fiercely. And now the Lord starts cursing again, which was the third time. "You are cursed from the earth, and when you till the ground, it shall not henceforth yield to you her strength: and a fugitive and a vagabond shall you be on the earth."

Here the Lord brings up farming again when he says to Cain "when you till the ground."

In Genesis 2:5, it says, "And there was not a man to till the ground." The Lord told Adam, "Cursed is the ground for your sake."

Now we come to John, who had the audacity to make the following statement in John 3:12. He said, "We should love one another." That's for sure, and certainly we should love one another. Now John continues, "Not as Cain, who was of that wicked one, and slew his brother." Did he do so deliberately?

"And wherefore slew he him. Because his works were evil." Please let me know how his works were evil and his brother's righteous. This is gross coming from John. He probably never read this portion of the Bible. It seems he heard the consensus taken up about Cain in general; however, he never analyzed the details.

Cain's works were evil, according to John, and Abel's were right. All Abel did was offer a lamb, while Cain offered produce, and the Lord did not like the produce. And He showed He had no use for it.

In essence, it was the Lord who handled this in a nonsensible way. If He had said to the two brothers something like, "That was nice of you boys, offering me the fruit of your labor, and I accept from both of you your offerings." But in this instance, the Lord shows He is not much of a psychiatrist. If it had happened that way, then the story would not have been in the Bible at all.

No, God liked the meat better and therefore made it an issue with the consequence that Abel died.

John did not say a word about Lamech, who killed two people and bragged about it, though they were not his brothers (Genesis 4:23). So, it is all right to kill people as long as you do not kill your brother? But John has a tendency to talk about things he never researched, like the previously mentioned situation and when he says a couple times that nobody has seen God. Everybody has been told this story from when they were a child to adulthood. With consequences, one knows the story of Cain and Abel at faith value. But has anybody ever looked at the real issue? No, God took sides, which was His prerogative, but was it the right one?

The dialogue between the Lord and Cain continued.

Cain said to the Lord, "My punishment is greater than I can bear. Behold you have driven me out this day from the face of the earth, and I shall be a fugitive and a vagabond: and it shall come to pass, that every one that finds me shall slay me."

Who is everyone? So far, only his father and mother were alive. Adam and Eve did not have any other kids. *Adam and Eve were* not about to slay their oldest and now their only son, particularly, as they were not even close to being everyone!

"And the Lord said to Cain, therefore whoso ever slays Cain, vengeance shall be taken on him seven-fold." That was not much help for Cain, because than he would be dead. This indicates that at that time, one could expect slayings, but from "whoso ever"? Otherwise, God would not have said "whoso ever"! Again, this indicates multiple people!

"And the Lord put a mark on Cain, lest any finding him should kill him." Again, who is "any"? This indicates there must have been quite a few people around besides Adam and Eve, most likely people who lived in the surrounding countries.

When I was about eleven or twelve years old, I asked a preacher about this and he told me those were the people yet to come about. And I regrettably accepted that. If this was true, then Cain would not have had to worry about being killed. Because all those people in the future would not know what had happened and they would not be all that interested in the episode with Cain. It would not have been so scary for Cain that he had to ask the Lord for mercy right there and then, because Cain feared all the people living around him.

Genesis 4:16 says, "And Cain went out from the presence of the Lord, and dwelt in the land of Nod, on the east of Eden."

Where and what is that land of Nod? Again, here is mention of on the east of Eden?

Luckily for him, he found a girl there! And she became his wife. And Cain knew his wife and she had a son. They named him Enoch.

And Cain did build a city and named the city after his son Enoch. So the part about cursing the ground obviously had no effect upon him.

There were quite a few people living in the land of Nod already. And all those people could not have been created by God. There were plenty of people to build that city, among other cities, for.

What Cain did is recorded in Genesis 4:17. "And Cain found himself a wife in the land of Nod." It looks like he became an honored and likable man out there, which is a far cry from being a fugitive and a vagabond, which is a man fleeing from the law, a transient, a tramp, one who wanders from place to place. It sure does not look like Cain was all of the above. And we can observe that from all indications it is certain Cain never became a repeat offender. He did not kill again, and the punishment of being cursed from the earth had no bearing on Cain, because he was not a farmer anymore. He also married a girl who was not one of the Lord's creations. And he had a son Enoch, who had Irad. Irad had Mehujael, and he had Methusael. He had Lamech. And Lamech had a son, and he called him Noah. We will learn more about Noah in a later chapter.

This was the genealogy of Cain in the land of Nod.

"And Lamech took himself two wives." He just took them, for marriage was not known in this time period. He was the first recorded man in history who had more than one wife.

Later on, in the Bible, it is recorded that there were kings who had hundreds of concubines, which were second wives to the king but were not "married" to him. They were free to have sex with them whenever they chose and whenever they wanted.

Judges 8:30–31 says, "Gideon had three score and ten sons of his body begotten: for he had many wives. And his concubine, she also bore him a son."

Lamech appeared to be a bully and a bragger. He killed two men, one for wounding him and another one for hurting him. Let's hope that poor guy did not just hurt Lamech's feelings and therefore lost his life. But Lamech started bragging to his wives about his killings. And he was quite proud of them too.

However, John, in the book of John, never said, "We should love each other, but not like Lamech!"

Anyway, the Lord did nothing to Lamech, who killed two people, probably because killings were commonplace by then, and the Lord did not care anymore. Their blood was not crying to heaven. And it was in a strange country.

Well, at least the Lord did not start cursing again, this time about Lamech. Inconsistency seems to be one of His traits. Or He just overlooked the whole deal. Please observe that in the whole story of Cain, it is the Lord who handles everything and not God.

However, the offspring from Cain was Enoch. And it is continued, "And unto Enoch was born Irad: and Irad begat Mehujael: and Mehujael begat Methusael and Methusael begat Lamech" (Genesis 4:18).

Now, in Genesis 4, Adam got Seth, and in Genesis 5:18, there appeared another Enoch and Enoch had a son Methusalah. Methusalah had Lamech. So, was Enoch a son from Cain or an offspring from Seth? And where did Lamech come from?

As biblical history shows, there could not have been a creation when there were already many people around in the land of Nod and in many more lands. This includes Eden. Why would God create existing countries like Egypt and Ethiopia and others? Besides, archeologists have found skeletons from people and animals more than one hundred million years old in Africa and other places on earth!

Here are more details about Eden and surrounding countries.

In Genesis 2:8, it says, "And the Lord God planted a garden eastward in Eden."

So, from this statement, we can conclude that there was already a place or territory by the name of Eden in existence. Otherwise, it would have sufficed to say, "And the Lord planted a garden, period."

In Genesis 4:16, we read eastward of Eden, the Lord made the Garden of Eden. And the land of Nod was again to the east of Eden—where people did exist. They were living there already before the creation of Adam; however, they were not aware of an existing God! How could they be?

Genesis 2:11, 13, and 14 describes the situation further. "And a river went out of Eden." This river did not go out of the Garden of Eden, because this river started out of a place named Eden, and from there, it went to the Garden of Eden, to water it. From there, it was parted into four heads, indicating Eden was already an existing place. "The name of the first head is Pison, which compasses [surrounds] the whole land of Havilah." The whole land of Havilah! This was known for its gold. We have another existing land, where there was gold, bdellium, and onyx stone. Adam, for sure, would not have been all that interested in gold and precious stones; he would not have had a clue about what gold and precious stones were, but the people living there certainly knew there was gold, and they were in possession of it and had already found onyx and probably other semiprecious stones. This country was already known for its gold and onyx by people living there. And in all probability, they were making jewelry too.

"And the second river is Gihon." This one encompasses the whole land of Ethiopia, which is south of Egypt and still is. Another existing country is mentioned here. If the world was just created, then why are Ethiopia and Egypt existing countries mentioned here?

"And the third river is Hiddekel, which goes toward the east of Assyria," and then last, God brings up the Euphrates, which is also an existing name. How much proof does one need that there were numerous countries all around Eden and all with inhabitants before the creation, like the land of Nod. How convenient for God to create a world with countries and rivers that were already in existence and named by people.

In Genesis 25:18, a statement is made, when Ismael, who was Hagar's and Abraham's son, died. "And they dwelt from Havilah unto Shur, that is before Egypt, as thou goes toward Assyria." This all sounds familiar.

In 1 Samuel 15:7, we read, again existing peoples. "And Saul smote the Amelekites from Havilah until thou come to Shur, that is over against Egypt." Those countries are mentioned as lands or countries with how many people living there already? If God was the first one to make human beings, why then did He mention all those existing countries with people in them? This means the creation was a hoax? Because those countries were there already! It becomes incomprehensible how God named those rivers and to what lands they were streaming if there were no people already living there. Then later those countries and rivers would have gotten names from the people living there and not beforehand.

We have no idea how many people already lived in Eden, Ethiopia, Havilah, Egypt, Nod, and Assyria.

So, we know now as a fact that Eden was also occupied by people long before God created Adam. Why were all those places mentioned here for everybody to see, but nobody mentioned them or brought them to our attention?

No, sir, churches don't want to have their apple carts upset. For sure, these countries and rivers must have already existed, because it is mentioned in the creation story over and over. Everybody who reads the Bible reads right over this without paying attention to the details, but some say they did read the Bible from the beginning to the end, without realizing what it said. Some did not want to talk about it, or if they did, they were silenced.

So, the Bible shows through transparency that there were already people living on earth, before God "created" the earth. Again, the land of Nod is mentioned; it is where Cain got his wife. If Cain had not found a wife there, then probably the land of Nod would not have been mentioned, even though the country of Nod was already in existence before the creation.

Now we can deduct from these data that the creation story is just a story.

CHAPTER 7

The Sons of God

We never hear of a female God, except in the Mormon religion, which proclaims that there is a Mrs. God, which makes some sense, in respect to Genesis 6:1 and 2. Remember we could see in the creation of Adam that the Gods were hermaphrodites. But now we are talking about the sons of God. So, the Mormons think if he had sons, then there must have been a female God.

Genesis 6:1–4 says, "And it came to pass, when men began to multiply on the face of the earth, and daughters were born unto them, that the sons of God saw the daughters of men that they were fair and they [the sons of God, that is] took them wives of all which they chose."

In the Revised Bible, it says, "The sons of God married the daughters of man." This sounds more civilized than "taking them of all which they chose." Nevertheless, they must have married as many as they chose.

However, marriage was not known in those days! Even hundreds of years later, for instance in Abraham's days, they still did not marry. So, the verse in the new revised Bible becomes obviously an inaccurate printing of the story.

This is what happened when Rebekah came to Isaac to meet him for the first time Genesis 24:67: "And Isaac brought her in his mother Sarah's tent, and he took Rebekah, and she became his wife; and he loved her: and Isaac was comforted after his mother's death." Still no marriage here, Isaac just took her, just like the sons of God did. And still no wedding here.

In Genesis 6:4, we continue with the sons of God. "There were giants in the earth. In those days, and also after that, when the sons of God came in unto the daughters of men, and they bear children to them, the same [those children], became mighty men, which were of old, men of renown."

You could expect that if you had a father who was a son of God! As I said earlier, marriage did not exist, because they just took them. In those days, marriage was unheard of and not established yet, except in the New International Version where they married, but by whom? There were no priests yet in existence, so who could marry those sons of God? This shows that the new Bible translations make this story more civilized but not true.

Here is more interesting news about the sons of God. Job 1:6 says, "Now there was a day when the sons of God came to present themselves before the lord." Do observe it does not say here the sons of God came to present themselves before God their father. No, they came to present themselves before the Lord. This indicates that God and the Lord are two different deities.

Job 2:1 says, "There was a day when the sons of God came again to present themselves before the lord." This was the second time they presented themselves to the Lord.

And in Romans 8:14, we read, "For as many as are led by the spirit of God, they are the sons of God." Only in a figurative way are they sons of God when they are led by the spirit and not literally.

However, if the sons of God came to present themselves to the Lord, then there is no spirit of God who makes those sons sons of God, because they are and then go to heaven to present themselves to the Lord.

Romans 8:19 says, "For the earnest expectation of the creature waits for the manifestation of the sons of God."

Where did God's only begotten son come from if there were already sons of God? This can be explained. Of all the sons God Himself had, he only had one by a daughter of men. That is by Maria. This had to be a son because a daughter would not have had the same effect as a son had overall in the Bible. We never hear about "daughters of God"! There are no daughters of God, because all the sons are hermaphrodites (bisexual), just like their father. But they discovered girls on earth, and they did like them better, just like human boys do. And God's sons had sex with them and did get offspring.

Now they were sons of God, which explains how their offspring were renowned. In other words, they were very smart and wise. This again becomes obvious and understandable when you know your father is a son of God.

There is one more reference to the sons of God. Job.38:7 says, "When the morning stars sang together, and all the sons of God shouted for joy."

With all this information, we can see that God had many sons. However, Jesus was different in respect that He was born from God and a human as a human being.

CHAPTER 8

God, the Lord, and Noah

Matthew 24:37–38 says, "But as the day of Noe [Noah] was, so shall also the coming of the son of man be. For as in the days that were before the flood, they were eating and drinking" [What's wrong with that? Everybody has to eat and drink to stay alive. Marrying and giving away in marriage, until the day that Noah entered into the ark [Again, what is wrong with that? Marrying was unheard of in those days; it is not until hundreds of years later we read in the Bible about marriage. Isaac took Rebecca in his mother's tent. And they became a pair. Well, we can see no reason to destroy the whole earth because of eating and drinking and marrying for reasons as given by Jesus the Christ himself.]"

This is what the Bible says about the time of Noah in Genesis 6:5: "And God saw that the wickedness of man was great on the earth, and that every imagination of the thoughts of his heart was only evil continuously." Was it because they were eating and drinking and marrying and giving away in marriage as Jesus said? Jesus had a different view on the situation than the Lord God had. It repented the Lord that he had made man on earth, and it grieved him at his heart. Because the Lord could not see beforehand the consequences of creating the earth?

Now we come to the official story of Noah.

Next, we start out with to two deities giving conflicting orders. Those are again God and the Lord.

In Genesis 6:19, God instructs Noah, "Of every living thing of all flesh, **two** of every sort shall you bring into the ark they shall be male and female. Of fowls, cattle and of every creeping thing of the earth, two of every sort shall come unto thee, to keep them alive." Well, everybody knows that of each animal, only two, the male and the female, were going into the ark. Two of every creeping thing of the earth? How is Noah going to comply with that?

There was no special delivery available to get the animals from what is now Australia, South and North America, the North and South Poles, or even animals from China and for that matter Europe too. Besides that, those animals have to eat too to stay alive. And every animal has to live in its own environment, temperature-wise, which is very important for them, like in the ice regions of the north and south poles. Others live in humid or even very high humidity conditions, and some can only survive at high altitudes.

Consequently, those animals from those special environments could not survive for long in the desert areas and certainly not in an enclosed area like in the ark for over a year!

Genesis 6:22 tells us, "Thus did Noah according to all that God commanded him, so he did."

According to the Bible, first, it was God who gave the command to Noah to take of each animal a male and a female into the ark.

Now, the Lord comes into the picture again, and we will look at what the Lord's command to Noah was. Then if we read further, we'll see that now it is the Lord who is giving all the conflicting commands to Noah.

Genesis 7: 1–3, and 5 says, "And the Lord said to Noah: 'of every clean beast you shall take to thee by **sevens.** [Not by twos, as God had instructed Noah, but now the Lord said: by sevens.] The clean beasts by **sevens** the male and his female, that is seven males and seven females and of beasts that are not clean by two, the male and his female. Also, the fowls of the air by sevens, the male and the female; to keep their seed alive upon the face of all the earth...

And Noah did according to everything the Lord commanded him."

Did he really now? Now he does what the Lord commanded him also? Earlier, He had already done what God commanded him. Now Noah did put seven of every animal that was clean in the ark.

Later when we read on, we see that Noah put into the ark two animals of each sort. So, he did not according to everything the Lord commanded him, to put seven of each into the ark, but what God had told him earlier, by putting two of each in the ark!

Genesis 7:7 says, "And Noah and his family went into the ark, because of the waters of the flood." This was the first time that they went into the ark.

Now another error the Lord made; later God made the same mistake. "Of clean beasts, and of beasts that are not clean, and of fowls ..." (Genesis 7:8).

Genesis 7: 9–10 continues, "They went in two and two unto Noah in the ark as God had commanded him. [This was the second time they went into the ark with two of each animal as God had commanded him.] And it came to pass after seven days that the waters of the flood were upon the earth." This means they were already in the ark seven days before the rain started.

Genesis 7:12–13 says, "And the rain was upon the earth forty days and forty nights. In the selfsame day entered Noah and his family in the ark." This is the third time they went in!

Genesis 7:15 says, "And they went in unto Noah in the ark, two and two of all flesh, wherein is the breath of life." The fourth time?

And in Genesis 7:16, we read, "And they went in, as God commanded him," and this time not as the Lord or not even as God Himself commanded the first time. There must have been quite a few times that they went in.

So, God had the last word after all, and all the Lord could do was shut them in. Now we know again that there are two different

Gods at work here, God and the Lord, who shut them in. God did not shut them in, but the Lord did.

But that was not all, because the Lord told Noah, "You shall take of every clean beast, the male and his female to thee by sevens, the male and his female: and of beasts that are not clean by two, the male and his female" (Genesis 7:8).

Now God Himself is getting confused. He also starts talking about clean and not clean beasts. "Of clean beasts, and of beasts that are not clean, and of fowls, and of everything that creeps on the earth" (Genesis 7:8).

"There went in two and two unto Noah. As God had commanded." But here God starts to talk about clean beasts also, just like the Lord did! Not that it made any difference. Because now "Noah did put in the ark two and two of all flesh where in is the breath of life"—not sevens. So, it made no difference if they were clean or not.

Hundreds of years later, Moses and Aaron told the Israelites, on orders of the Lord, which animals were considered to be clean and unclean. At the time, the Israelites were going through the desert for a duration of forty years (Leviticus 11:1–47). No way Noah could know what clean beasts were at this time.

But it came all out in the wash, because now it was just two by twos, clean or unclean. However, Noah could not have had the slightest idea of what a clean beast was. Maybe he was under the impression that he had to give them a bath first to make them all clean.

Genesis 6:3 says, "And the Lord said, my spirit shall not always strive with man, yet his days shall be 120 years." This can be interpreted as the time needed for Noah to build the ark, one hundred and twenty years. And then God was going to wipe out the world.

God is the one who instructed Noah to build the ark as follows: Make the ark 300 cubits long by 50 cubits wide by 30 cubits high, which is equivalent to 450 feet long by 75 feet wide by 45 feet high, with one window, one cubit square. This is 1.5 feet by 1.5

feet. Not much of a window. And put an entrance door in the side, no size given, and make the whole contraption three stories.

The window did not have glass in it because they did not know yet about glass, so it was a piece of wood that could be opened by pushing it out from the bottom and then up, sliding it sideways, or taking it out completely if the need was there, but most of the time, the rain would prevent that.

In the new translations of the Bible, it is conveniently written as a whole row of windows. This is not according to the original Bible. It is changed in the new translation, and they are making a correction and improvement in God's design. This indicates that God did not know what He was doing when He designed the ark, according to the new translation. But originally, it was one 1.5-foot-by-1.5-foot window, as recorded in all the original Bibles.

God's design was not all that great. Did God make an error when and how He instructed Noah to build the ark? It would not be the first time He made an error. Noah was told to make one window, period.

In Genesis 6:17, God speaks: "And behold, I, even I, do bring a flood of waters upon the earth, to destroy all flesh, where in is the breath of life: and everything that is in the earth shall die" (by drowning!).

The animals did not sin, so why did they have to drown and die? Was it because God wanted to wipe out everything on earth, even all the ones he supposedly created, all those innocent animals?

Well, let's face it; God could have wiped out, that is killed, supposedly everybody on earth by whatever means, except for Noah's family. There would not have been need for the ark without them. But then God would have come across as a killer so He chose to do it with the ark so He did not kill, but the flood did. In other words, He easily could have come up with a more humane way to wipe out life on earth, being omnipotent! And He would not have to have been sorry afterward either.

God appears to be not much of an animal lover, and for the humans, He did not show much compassion either in spite of the Lord later saying He felt sorry about everything that had happened and what He had done!

Genesis 8:21 says, "And the Lord said in his heart, I will not again curse the ground any more: neither will I again smite any more everything living, as I have done." Here it shows He had cursed again. Not becoming of a God. Nevertheless, He had done it!

There is a printed excerpt from a conference on February 23 and 24, 2007, which was held at the Second Baptist Church, where is not given, but it was probably in Houston.

Dr. Ross, talking about God, states, "God has care and love for his creation." Does He know, Dr. Ross? Looking at Noah's story, the opposite is true.

In Genesis 6:6, we read, "And it repented the Lord that He had made man on the earth, and it grieved Him at His heart." This does not show much love for His creation! Now Genesis 6:7 says, "And the Lord said, I will destroy man who I have created from the face of the earth, both man and beast, and the creeping thing, and the fowls of the air, which is everything!" In other Words, "I am sorry that I have created them!"

Wow! How much care and love does He show here for His creation?

God and the Lord never cared much about animals, except when they were offered on an altar. Then He always savored the smell of the burning meat.

Here is an example of Him not caring for animals.

Deuteronomy 13:15 says, "Destroy that city, and all that is in there, and the cattle [livestock] thereof, with the edge of the sword."

What did the cattle do?

Again, he certainly does not show much love for His creation, now does He?

This is most of the time.

This shows religion is quite capable of changing things around, while whitewashing things out of the Bible, so it will look better than it actually is, just to placate the congregation or the masses. Then, to them, it sounds good. The masses like to hear what they want to hear even if it is not true. One can pacify a congregation so they feel good about it and make them believe whatever you say, because it is human nature to believe everything we want to hear, and this way they feel good about it so they can agree with it, even if it is not true.

Back to Noah.

Now imagine the smell from the animals and their excrement in a completely enclosed environment. The excrement alone would add up to such an amount of feces in 318 days, that the ark could not carry it for long, besides all the urine being added to the waste. The ark was sealed with pitch, inside and outside.

And what did Noah's party of eight do with all their human waste? Throw it out of the window? Or just add it to the animals' waste? Only the smell would have been terrible. Maybe they got used to it or the Lord made it so that it did not smell? No, He did not, because at the end, all of a sudden, He remembered Noah.

After a few weeks, the level of urine on the bottom level alone would be prohibitive, because they would have to wade through it and the animals would have gotten all kinds of diseases while standing in the urine or lying in it. Now try to live in it for more than a year! The people who took care of the animals would also have to wade through it day in and day out in a pitch-dark environment to feed them.

Besides, with no ventilation except the 1.5-foot-square window, the stench would have been awful. Even if Noah opened the window, all the animals would have died, including Noah and his family, because methane gas would have filled the whole ark. And it is explosive to boot.

Now the problem of getting those animals water is a different issue. Animals have to drink quite a bit and constantly. There was plenty of water outside the ark because of all the rain. Did He have to store the tons of water inside too? For over a year? How could he? They had not made holding tanks yet. They could not bathe themselves either all this time. There were no pipes to get water to the animals, in spite of all the salt water outside, which would not have done them any good anyway.

Noah, his sons, and their wives could not carry all the water to the animals, because it was pitch-dark inside the ark and they could not light a flame because of the methane gas; besides, the strong odor would have prohibited them from attending the animals after a while. There was no ventilation through the ark!

It makes me wonder how Noah got the polar bears, penguins, and reindeer to come from the polar regions all the way to the Middle East, and the same goes for all the types of bears, like black bears, grizzly bears, brown bears, Kodiak bears, koalas, and pandas, just to name a few, and the buffalo and all types of deer, like reindeer, elk, and caribou, to name a few more. Then there were other animals, like all sort of snakes—the rattlers, cobras, anaconda, coral snakes, pythons, and many others, including the ones that lived in South and North America, Africa, India, and Australia, where there are also kangaroos, dingoes, ostriches, llamas, and so on. What about elephants, wooly mammoths, saber-toothed tigers, and dinosaurs? What about the chimpanzees, orangutans, gorillas, rhesus monkeys, baboons, and gibbons and many more types of apes and monkeys?

And did Noah get all the different types of parrots? Even if Noah could get his hands on one kind of parrot, then that pair of parrots would have never developed into all the tens of other unbelievably beautiful types of parrots— unless we go by Darwin's theory!

And how about all the different species of apes, all after their kind, as Noah was ordered. If Noah had taken a pair of apes, no matter what kind, you really think they would have developed again into all the species as we know now?

And what of all the animals that creep on the earth? The millions of different insects, fleas, flies, bees, mosquitoes, butterflies, and bats, just to name a few. These creatures are very, very delicate. Granted, butterflies could have been larvae or eggs at the time, but in a year's time, they would have evolved into butterflies and then what?

All the types of dinosaurs were probably more than the ark could handle.

This would have been impossible. Because we can figure out, there definitely would not have been room enough in the ark to accommodate and store all those critters—a total of eight thousand and two of each makes sixteen thousand, according to estimates of what was around at the time.

Now religion says God could have made them all hibernate during the cruise, and maybe the eight humans did also. But look at all the room needed for food supplies necessary to feed all those animals and humans for more than a year.

Genesis 6:21 says, "And God said: take to you of all food that is eaten, and gather it to you; and it shall be for food for you and them [the animals] thus no hybernation." So here we have orders to get all the food that is eaten. In spite of religion claiming that God might have made them hibernate. Then there would not have been need for Noah to gather food. Then we might as well say that the Lord had the humans hibernate too.

Can you imagine all the hay, fruits, and nuts, plus all the other types of food needed for all the animals? What did the tigers, lions, and snakes eat, for example—in spite of them being vegetarians on orders of God? (See Genesis 1:30, "And it was so.")

And think of the provisions needed for Noah and his family, all eight of them, for over one year (more than twelve months) and with no refrigeration available! However, everybody was supposed to be a vegetarian!

Just like the sailors in the Middle Ages and later, when those sailors were too long at sea, they got beriberi and scurvy, diseases created by the lack of certain vitamins and fresh vegetables and fruit. Quite a few sailors in those days aboard sailing ships contracted them and died because of too much time spent at sea without fruits and vegetables.

So, you think there was no spoilage? Storage would have been a problem for sure.

All those earlier mentioned species supposedly died off? From what and when?

We can deduct there was most likely no flood in the Americas, Asia, Africa, Australia, and Europe. There were humans living in South and North America, Europe, Asia, and Africa before and after the flood, according to archeologists, like Aborigines, Aztecs, African tribes, Japanese, and Chinese, and who knows who else? From all indications, if there was a flood, then it must have been a tremendous local flood, definitely not over the whole wide world, only in Asia Minor.

Now in Josh. 24:14 "The Gods your fathers served that were on the other side of the flood and in Egypt".(KJ) "On the other side of the flood", indicates a dry side!

This indicates there must have been a local flood only.

The NIV changed "the other side of the flood": to "the other side of the river". So as far as they are concerned, there is no reference now to the flood

It can be established, as mentioned earlier, and it will come up again and again, that God is interested only in Asia Minor and His people there.

The ark landed.

In Genesis 7:11, we read that the rain started in the six-hundredth year of Noah's life and in the seventeenth day of the second month that year. So, it was Noah's birthday maybe? In Genesis 8:13–14, it tells us that one year later, in the six hundred and first year of Noah's life, on January 1, the waters were dried up. That's amazing! All that water was gone. Two months later, in the second month, on the twenty-seventh day, the ground was reported dry again or still dry. How about that?

Up to the day that God told Noah he could get out of the ark, they spent 365 days and 10 more days, plus the 7 days they spent in the ark before it started to rain, for a total of 382 days. So, they were cooped up in the ark for all those days.

Genesis 7:17 and 24 tell us, "It rained for forty days, day and night, and all the water upon the earth prevailed one hundred and fifty days." So, after the forty days of rain, the water prevailed for 150 days. After that, the waters abated. But it took more than a year in total before they could leave the ark.

Genesis 8:4–5 says, "And the ark landed on Mount Ararat in the seventh month. [Now it was six months or 180 days that everybody was cooped up in the ark.] And the waters decreased continually until the tenth month and the tops of the mountains were seen." Now we are at about 270 days.

Genesis 8:13–14 says, "And it came to pass that after 11 months, that is about 330 days, the waters were dried up from the earth, and Noah looked, and behold the waters were dried up and the ground was dry! And in the next year on the second month on the 27th day the earth dried." The ground was dry already, but now the ground dried again. And now God gave the command to Noah to get everybody out of the ark. Thus, they were in the ark for more than a year, 365 days total plus 17 days.

Most trees and plants cannot exist that long in water. The cactus family would have been extinct for sure. And most likely, most of the trees that can't tolerate water constantly for that long, including olive trees. Maybe some of the swamp trees could. Not likely. But for sure not oak trees, chestnuts, maples, pine trees, fir trees, magnolias, and a lot more.

And where did all the water go after it stopped raining? It could not go into the oceans, the seas, or into the lakes, because they were already underwater too, being the low points on the earth.

Can you imagine all oceans (147,550 million square miles), the seas (7,498,200 square miles), and all the lakes having thousands of feet of water above sea level? That is if the flood was worldwide.

It would have taken many years or at least many lifetimes for all that water to evaporate. It would probably still be here. There surely would be evaporation, but then we have rain again too. So, we can deduct from this that as earlier mentioned, the flood was only local to that area in Asia Minor and surrounding areas.

In 2008, there was a flood from the rivers in Iowa and in all the low-lying cities, and from there, the water went down the Mississippi River, flooding every city downstream. This was only a very little flood compared to the big flood. However, as relatively small as it was, it still took more than four weeks to get rid of the floodwater. It is obvious that all the rainwater must have mixed with the salt water during the flood, only in Asia Minor alone. There is the Mediterranean, the Black Sea, the Persian Gulf, the Red Sea, the Caspian Sea, and the Dead Sea to name a few. They all mixed with all the fresh water from the rain. The water then becomes brackish. Most vegetation does not tolerate brackish water.

In 1950, when there was a big flood in the Netherlands, the farmland became unusable because of the brackish water, and the farmers did have to treat their land extensively with chemicals to correct the situation.

Genesis 7:19 says, "And all the high hills that were under the whole heaven were covered." Another reference to a flat earth? "Upwards to fifteen cubits above the mountains were covered" (Genesis 7:20). One cubit equals 1.5 feet. Fifteen cubits equals 22.5 feet. So, 22.5 feet above the mountains did the waters prevail, and the mountains were covered.

Confusing statements are made here. First, the high hills were covered and then 22.5 feet more, and the mountains were covered in water. Obviously, the writers of the Bible were not aware of the high mountains in the Himalayas and the Andes, just to mention a few.

Genesis 7:21 says, "And all flesh died that moved on the earth. And every man all in whose nostrils was the breath of life, all that were in the dry land, died."

Genesis 7:22 continues, "And every living substance was destroyed, upon the face of the earth." Something to be proud of?

And what kinds of mountains are mentioned here? Mount Everest?

Consider now that all the high peaks are in the Himalayas, in India and the Andes, as mentioned earlier. Well, at least it appears there was enough water to float the ark, if there ever was one.

Yet trees and plants, even cacti, are still growing nowadays. Cacti would have become extinct, so did it really happen? One wonders. If Noah brought seeds from every tree and plant in the world into the ark, then they could still be existing. However, there are some special and exotic trees peculiar only to India, the rain forest, New Zealand, Australia, and even Canada.

However, He did not get such orders from God or the Lord. Even if Noah had gotten such instructions, Noah could never have complied. Who would have acquired all the seeds for him? In spite of having 120 years to acquire them, they did not know at this time that the Americas even existed, besides Australia and China and Europe and the North and South Poles!

Now in Genesis 8:5, we are informed that after the rain stopped (after 234 days) the tops of the mountains could be seen.

Genesis 8:6 says, "However at the end of forty days Noah opened *the window* of the ark he had made." Quite confusing statements are made here.

The NIV states here also that Noah opened *the window*, Noah had made.

However, when God gave instructions to build the ark in Genesis 6:14 and 15. Than there is no mentioning of making a window like in the King James Bible, which even gives dimensions of the window.

By whom could the tops of the mountains be seen? They certainly could not see Mount Everest or the Andes from where they were. Probably and most likely, they did see some tops from the Ararat Mountains.

According to the Bible (Genesis 8:4), the ark landed on Mount Ararat. Mountains are quite high, from hundreds to tens of thousands of feet high. Mount Ararat is around sixteen thousand feet high and in Turkey.

Again, where did all that water go? Was the water as high as the mountains? If that was the height of the water, everything was underwater for at least sixteen thousand feet, including all the oceans, seas, lakes, and rivers.

Besides, they were quite a long way from home, in Turkey. Can you imagine? They were at the time the only ones on earth, as the story goes, when they went out of the ark. There was nobody to ask for directions. They did not have a compass either. They could not see Mount Ararat all the way from where they used to be living, so they could not use that as a reference point.

Genesis 8:20 says, "And Noah did build right there an altar unto the Lord: And took of every clean beast, and of every clean fowl and offered them on an altar." With what? With no wood to burn? Maybe they salvaged wood from the ark? So here we are also confronted again with clean animals.

Again, how did he know which ones were clean? He might have made some animals extinct by doing that unless they reproduced while in the ark, and that would have been under unbelievably harsh conditions.

Now picture this; where are we? You have no idea where in the world you are. Up to a minimum of five hundred miles from home and nobody to ask for directions? Which way is home? They had no idea if they had to go north, south, east, or west to the place where they had lived. And if they made it back, there was nobody to greet them or to make them feel at home again. Everybody was gone. And where did they live from during the time they were trying to find their way back through the mud? There was absolutely nothing to eat. No wheat or plant protein was available. They were still vegetarians. The only way they could have survived for a while would be by fishing. However, they were still vegetarians. No fish allowed. Only herbs.

And where did the animals live from when they came out of the ark, when they were free again. They started hunting for food. There was nothing to find for them, except some of the animals that were in the ark. Can you imagine how skinny they must have been? But even the animals were still vegetarians on orders of the Lord.

However, rabbits do reproduce prolifically. So, there might have been an abundance of rabbits, guinea pigs, rats, and mice for a while, but how about all the other animals? Besides that, every beast of the earth was also supposed to be a vegetarian! (Genesis 2:30).

Up to Noah's time, they were still supposed to be vegetarians. Not a word about it in the Bible. It certainly would have made an interesting story to hear how they made it back. All it says in the Bible, in Genesis 9:20, is "And Noah began to be a husband man, and he planted a vineyard." From what? For whom? Maybe as a hobby?

Now observe the strange story about Noah.

Genesis 9: 21–25 tells how Noah got drunk sampling his wine, and he was without clothes in his tent. In other words, he made himself comfortable while naked. It is known that he had three sons—Shem, Ham, and Japheth. And Ham was the middle son and father of Canaan. "And Noah begat three sons, Shem, Ham and Japheth. And Ham is the father of Canaan" (Genesis 9:18).

Ham saw his father naked. He must have gone to Noah's tent and said, "Dad, how are you doing?" There was no answer, and he went inside. There he found him naked. Now Ham went to his two brothers and told them about their father being nude in the tent asleep.

The two brothers walked backward into the tent, carrying a garment on their shoulders, and so covered him without seeing their father's nakedness. They also could have left Noah there as he was until he woke up, and then Noah could have dressed himself, unless they were afraid he would catch a cold lying there naked—very unlikely.

Noah awoke from his drunkenness, and he knew what his younger son had done to him. How could he know that? Did God may be inform him? (Genesis 9:24).

Obviously, he did not! First, he blamed his youngest son. It was the middle son, Ham. How would Noah know that Ham saw him naked? If that was what he was bitching about, then Shem and Japheth must have told Noah that he was naked. Or maybe he recognized the blanket.

In Genesis 9:25, Noah started again and said, "Cursed be Canaan; a servant of servants shall he be to his brothers." Still drunk? Sounds like it, because he should have said, "A servant shall he be to his uncles." He cursed his grandson Canaan. "Blessed be the Lord God of Shem, and Canaan shall be his servant, and Canaan shall be Japheth's servant also." What did Canaan do? So, the curse was Canaan shall be a servant to his brothers and not his uncles? Canaan was not even around during the incident! What a mix-up this was.

From all indications, Noah's reasoning was absurd. He most likely had a hangover and could not think straight because he, Noah, must have really enjoyed the wine. Probably had a headache to boot. So, he was looking for a culprit. Noah first blamed Japhet and then his grandchild Canaan.

Oh, come on now. Noah is responsible for himself. He was the one who got drunk and got naked. But he started cursing his grandchild, who probably did not have the slightest idea of what was going on, so instead of blaming himself, he instead blamed the grandchild, but he was definitely responsible for his own actions. And he made Canaan a servant for life to his uncles, but originally it was supposed to be his brothers, according to Noah.

It is human nature to always blame everything on somebody or something else, even if it is one's own doing and fault, which is exactly what Noah also did.

My mother, if something went wrong, always found a reason to blame it on someone or somebody, like us kids or even our dog. So, she never realized that it was her doing that caused the situation she was in.

Well, back to Noah while he was still in the ark.

At the end of forty days, when the rain stopped, Noah sent forth a raven, by opening the window of the ark, which he had made. God did not say by opening "a window." No, He said "the window," indicating there was only one window in the whole ark (Genesis 8:6).

This is obviously an oversight again by the translators of the Bible—the NIV and the new American Bible, Revised Edition—which call the window, "the hatch." According to the dictionary, a hatch is not even close to being a window. A hatch is an opening in the floor or deck or a door or gate with an opening above.

"And the raven went forth to and fro until the waters were dried up." For at least seven months, the raven kept flying? Ravens are not exactly amphibians. So, for more than a half year, the raven kept flying? What could he or she have lived on? Ravens are scavengers! Nothing was alive on the earth to eat supposedly. How did it propagate? There were only two ravens. And one was still in the ark.

If we look at the food habits of ravens, we find "common ravens are scavengers. They eat a wide array of animal foods, including arthropods, amphibians, small mammals, birds, reptiles, and carrion. They are attracted to carrion and eat also the insects that feed on carrion (chiefly on maggots and beetles)" (Boarman and Heinrich 1999).

So maybe the raven did find cadavers or what was left of them, still floating in the water. Very unlikely after a year because of fish having the time of their life while eating all those cadavers.

Next, he sent out a dove, but the dove returned because there was nothing solid to rest on.

Genesis 8:9 says, "For the waters were on the face of the whole earth. All water as far as the eye could see, except the ark." Seven days later, he sent the dove out again. That evening, the dove came back with an olive leaf in its mouth, which was plucked off. Plucked off from what?

Seven days earlier, it could not find a place to land on, not even an olive tree, because it was all water. A week later, there was an olive tree somewhere growing with leaves already on it. How strange.

Olive trees don't grow that much in one week, and they don't grow at higher altitudes either. This makes it more remarkable yet.

There was a flood as described in the Bible, and the whole earth was covered with water.

Genesis 7:18 says, "And the waters prevailed [became predominant] and were increased greatly upon the earth. So that the mountains were covered." It is pretty hard to comprehend the total amount of water involved. It absolutely boggles the mind. More than hundreds of trillions and more yet of gallons of water! Again, this would have taken more than a lifetime to evaporate.

In the beginning, everything was created according to the creation, and God saw it was good. Now in one swoop, He destroyed it all. And to top it off, God said He was sorry afterward. However, at the time of the creation, He saw everything was good!

In other words, He admits He made a mistake, and God promised He would never do it again (Genesis 8:21).

How do we know, when God makes a mistake with us, that He won't say, "Oops, I made a mistake. I'm sorry; I won't do that anymore or again"? It would probably be too late then anyhow. It becomes apparent that hurricanes, typhoons, tornados, lightning, and other calamities like earthquakes are caused by God, without regard for human life.

First, He was sorry about the creation (Genesis 6:6). Now, He is sorry about the destruction caused by the flood. What is next?

In Genesis 8:1, it says, "And God remembered Noah. [Lucky for Noah—otherwise, it would have been pretty gloomy for the man.] And God remembered every living thing and all the cattle that were with him in the ark, only cattle? And God made a wind to pass over the earth and the waters assuaged." This means the waters were less harsh and calmed. But they were lucky that God remembered Noah and every living thing and all the cattle, indicating that they were on their own all this time on the water when they were floating.

"All living things He did remember, and the cattle He remembered."

Floods do happen quite often all over the world, and lots of people die in them. We observed this quite recently when a tsunami occurred in the Indian Ocean, in Indonesia. The tsunami flooded and destroyed the coastal areas of a lot of countries, killing hundreds of thousands of natives and hundreds of tourists.

Local floods do occur quite often after persistent rains or at times when people start praying for rain during a drought, and then often it won't stop raining once it starts. It won't stop raining until there is a flood and everything is underwater. That is because everyone's mind then is tuned in to wanting and seeing it rain.

One prophet, according to the Bible, prayed for no rain, and it did not rain for three and a half years. This seems like overkill.

If God controls rain, then He also must control lightning, tornados, earthquakes, hurricanes, cyclones, and the many casualties that go with them. That's why we call them acts of God! And there is no Mother Nature we can blame it on, so the only other instigator is God Himself.

In Isaiah 45:7 and only in the new Bible, it says, "I make peace and I create disaster." So be it! All the other Bibles say, "I make peace and I create evil." Well, creating disasters is evil too. So now we know the Lord makes disasters like hurricanes, tornados, and earthquakes. We all know that tornados occur quite frequently, and hurricanes do also with all the dreaded, disastrous results. Thousands of humans have died because of these terrible acts of God. And everything is blamed on Mother Nature, which in essence is an act of the Lord. But God does not care anymore what happens to us. We are on our own.

According to scientists, we can expect when the ice melts in the North and South Poles, the oceans and seas will have their water levels rise to the extent that this time, it will create floods all over the world. Well, we will see.

CHAPTER 9

Noah Becomes the Savior of the World

Genesis 6:3 says, "It is written that the Lord said, 'my spirit shall not always strive with man.' [To *strive* is to make an earnest effort, to engage in strife, contend, or fight.] For that he also is flesh yet his days shall be a hundred and twenty years." What God is saying here is He gives men 120 years before He will destroy humankind. And at the same time, He will give Noah 120 years to build the ark.

Genesis 6:5 says, "And God saw that the wickedness of man was great on earth and the imagination of his thoughts was only evil, continuously." God thinks evil too but not continuously. Nevertheless, He knows and does evil too. This is shown in an earlier chapter.

Genesis 6:6 continues, "And it repented the lord that He had made man on the earth, and it grieved Him at his heart." To *repent* is to feel remorse or regret, as for something one has done or failed to do, according to the *Standard Encyclopedia Dictionary*. So, in essence what it says is God regretted that He made man on earth. In other words, He had made a mistake. He felt sorry He had created everything. He had made man on earth, and it grieved Him at His heart. So as far as the creation is concerned,

God considered it a fiasco. Is it just an expression, or does God have a heart also as we know it?

The Lord could not foresee how things would develop. The Lord wanted and expected everybody to do His bidding. But that did not happen. So He had not created perfect beings. He could have seen the handwriting on the wall after Adam, Cain, Lamech, and so on. Not a peep about Lamech, who is a bragger and killed left and right. But that's all right.

God could not control His subjects, and they did the wrong things—first, Adam, and then everybody in existence was committing violence and doing evil, according to God.

In Isaiah 45:7, God says, "I form the light and create darkness: I make peace and I create evil: I the Lord does all those things." Here He boasts of doing evil, and we can see that God admits that He does evil.

He wished He had never started the creation. And it repented the Lord that He had made man on earth and grieved Him at His heart (Genesis 6:6).

Genesis 6:7 says, "And the Lord said I will destroy man whom I have created from the face of the earth; both man, and beast … for it repented me that I have made them." And now He is ready to destroy *everybody*. He was losing control. All those people just did what they wanted to do and ignored God?

Not according to Jesus. He said in Matthew 25:38 the following: "For as in the days that were before the flood they were eating and drinking, marrying and giving in marriage until the day that Noah went in the ark."

If that was what the people did in those days, then that is weird, because it is still being done up to this day. What is wrong with eating and drinking? You have to do that to stay alive anyway. And what is wrong with marrying and giving in marriage? Besides that in those days before Noah and a long time after that, they just did not get married. Marriage was unheard of in those days, except in the NIV Bibles.

Much later, for instance, Isaac, one of Abraham's sons, took his girl in his mother's tent, and there he knew her. He did not marry her; he just took her, and she became his wife (Genesis 25:67). This is the first time that a saying from Jesus is outright questionable.

Well, we continue. Noah found grace in the eyes of the Lord. Good for humanity. God always finds at least one person who can save the world and humankind at the last minute. He had to find Noah; if not, then that would have been the end of the creation again as we know it.

First, God would have had to call it quits if Adam and his woman would have died after eating of the forbidden fruit, but they did not die. God told them, "You will surely die the day you eat from that tree." Everything then would have been destroyed from the earth. And now He does it again by threatening to wipe out everything. It makes one wonder if He does know what He is doing.

Second attempt to do it right, He made a new creation all over again.

Everything points now to the fact that the Gods wanted to try it one more time and start all over with everything done so far as the creation was concerned. Now we can see that according to the Lord, everything was a disaster up to then, and it grieved the Lord at His heart that He had made man on earth (Genesis 6:6). Yes, He said that.

As far as the creation is concerned, it was a disaster. Nothing worked out right. Too bad that the Gods could not see it coming when they started out with the creation—if there ever was a creation.

Again, this shows that the Gods do not know everything either, especially beforehand, and are not all-knowing or omniscient as we make them out to be.

In general, we give St. Nick more credit than God when we talk to our kids about good old St. Nick.

All the time, we say that God loves us, but that's only when it suits Him. He never said He did love us except for a few chosen ones. He liked Enoch, Noah, Abraham, Isaac, Jacob, Moses, Job, Daniel, and the prophets. But He had only three specific chosen ones; in other words, the following ones were His favorites: Noah, Daniel, and Job (Ezekiel 14:14). But boy oh boy if you do something He does not like!

All through the Old Testament, the Lord appears to be vengeful and always ready to punish by cursing and other means—besides laying down more than three hundred laws: "You shall do or not do this or that, or else, you die."

In Numbers 15:33–36 is a story about the Sabbath. A man was caught picking up wooden sticks, on the Sabbath, and they asked the Lord what should be done about this incident. And the Lord said to Moses, "The man shall be surely put to death: the entire congregation shall stone him with stones. And the congregation stoned him with stones, and he died."

What a merciful God we have here! The Lord said here that they should stone him with stones. What else but stones? One cannot stone, for instance, with marshmallows or pine cones. So why did He just not say, "Stone him"?

But the point is here God did not kill the man Himself. No, sir. If God knows everything, which in this instance He did not, because He had to be told, then He came out with a verdict. And the man died, as the Lord commanded Moses. He let other people do the dirty job.

We would probably run out of stones and people if we also dishonored the Sabbath, which we do! As serious as this is, we don't observe our Sunday at all—without any consequences.

And death for picking up some sticks on a Saturday or on a Sunday in the wilderness, which was in the desert? The death penalty for a minor offense?

But the point here is that God did not even know that there was a man who had gathered wood on the Sabbath. He had to be informed about the incident, and then He was asked what to do about it. Then He comes up with the death penalty! So, He could not kill that man Himself when that person flaunted His law? No, sir, because He was not even aware of it and He would not do it, period. This indicates again—and I say it over and over—God does not know before something happens. Only after it has happened does He know.

In conclusion, God chose Noah so He could clean the whole world of everybody in it and start a new world—conveniently all the people who were not created by Him from the beginning of the creation.

He picked Noah, not exactly the brightest guy around either. But it seems God did not have much to choose from; he was the only one available out of tens of thousands. Who knows how many there were at the time?

And He trusted him. But if Noah had not been there, then He was planning on wiping out each and every thing and there would have been only a world and a universe left and nobody to continue humanity!

Noah built the three-story high ark, with just one window and no ventilation, and pitch-dark inside. Unless you have had a chance to observe what goes on in a dairy farm, for one, the amount of cow manure and urine is greater than you would think possible. And those dairy farm animals are only cows. So, picture all the wet stuff coming down to the bottom level from above?

Imagine all the manure and urine from all the animals—the elephants, giraffes, buffalos, horses, all kinds of deer and bears, just to name a few.

Animals had to stand in it and lie down in the urine, with dire consequences as far as disease is concerned. Besides that, it was pitch-dark on each floor. Animals can't live too long at all in darkness and under conditions like that.

Imagine living in the pitch-dark for 375 days! Very few animals can live for long in total darkness. Only bats could. But they have to fly around to eat. And how did all those animals drink water?

So, the whole story is nice and interesting, but that is just what it is—an interesting story. It is not a true story as far as we can see, because animals were not capable of existing in the ark for any length of time. According to the Bible, they did for some 380 days. And Noah did not even know what clean and unclean beasts were. Yet he did all what God had commanded him Genesis 6:22. Then he did what the Lord commanded him again (Genesis 7:5), and a little bit later, he did it again as God had commanded him (Genesis 7:9 and again in Genesis 7:16). What kind of guy was Noah, supposedly obeying all those conflicting commands?

The only thing that is possible is that it was just a local flood in Asia Minor, not likely the whole earth! It says in Genesis 8:3 that the waters returned from the earth continually. That is impossible, because where did the water return to? The water was everywhere, and there were no low points anywhere. Rivers would not run, because there was nothing to run to. And all the ice caps and glaciers were underwater also and would start to melt. This created more water worldwide. So, all in all, it is not a very convincing story! Too many discrepancies and conflicting episodes.

There is documentation about a flood by another ancient country, which is almost similar to the story of Noah, except it does not have as many discrepancies as in the Noah story. It was written in the original Akkadian language on stone tablets and translated into Hittite and Hurrian, which were spoken at the time in Turkey and to the north of Mesopotamia. It is also known as the *Gilgamesh Epic*. However, this story was written before Noah's story, and it is alleged to have eventually made its way to the Holy Land. Then it was somehow copied into the Bible with dire consequences.

The story in the Bible has numerous discrepancies, indicating it could not have been written with inspiration of God, and if it was, than the inspiration was not all that accurate. So, from all indications, it looks more like data were copied and more wrong information was added.

CHAPTER 10

The Generations of Shem, Ham, and Japheth and the Gentiles

Genesis 10 tells us that right after the flood, the sons of Noah did get their offspring. However, they only recorded sons. Girls did not count in those days; they were just a by-product to acquire sons, it seems.

Genesis 10:5 says, "By these were the isles of the gentiles divided in their lands, every one after his tongue, their families, and in their nations."

Gentiles, among Jews, are those who are not Jews (*Standard Encyclopedic Dictionary*).

Webster's Dictionary defines *gentile* as a person of a non-Jewish nation or of non-Jewish faith.

We will come back to this issue in a moment.

In Genesis 10:20, it says, "These are the sons of Ham after their families, after their tongues, in their countries, and in their nations." And in Genesis 10:31, it says the same about the sons of Shem. Those are the sons of Shem, after their tongues, in their lands, after their nations. We are being told "after their tongues." This implies that they were speaking a different language or in a dialect. Each group spoke in their own tongue.

Dialects are hard to understand, even if you know the language.

The *Standard Encyclopedia Dictionary* defines *tongue* as a people or race, regarded as having their own language, a biblical use of the term.

Ham and his descendants lived after their tongues and in their countries. The same occurred with all the descendants from Shem. They also lived after their tongues and in their countries. Shem had five boys and twenty-one more boys from his five boys. One of his offspring was Eber. And Eber had two sons; the name of one was Peleg, for in his days the earth was divided. Only in his days? Divided into what?

The earth is still divided at present, into what is known as continents.

I bring it up again as far as descendants are concerned that girls don't seem to matter all that much, only the male line counted. Why?

Anyhow, the offspring from Shem, Ham, and Japheth became separate nations, after their families, after their tongues, in their lands (Genesis 10:20 and 31).

In Genesis 10:5, now we have the offspring from Japheth, and "by these were the isles of the gentiles (non-Jews) divided in their lands; every one after his tongue."

Did the offspring from Japheth become the non-Jews or gentiles? It does not say "these are the sons of Japheth, as it does say in verses 20 and 31 about Ham and Shem. So if it was not Japheth, then that means that there was a whole country of "gentiles, non-Jews" living on the isles, in their lands, indicating that the flood did not wipe them all out, the gentiles and everybody on earth. How else could there be a whole country with gentiles still living?

After listing all the descendants of Japheth, the text continues, "by these were the *isles of the gentiles* divided in their lands, *every one after his tongue*, their families, and in their nations."

So, it looks like the descendants from Japheth must have become the Gentiles? Those are non-Jews! If not, then there were a lot of Gentiles still living after the flood. So where did those Gentiles mentioned earlier come from? Everybody was supposedly wiped out in the flood. Now we are told there were actual survivors? Multiple nations, it says in Genesis 10:5.

God did not wipe out everybody as we are being told! How weird. What we can deduce from all this is that it must have been a local flood.

In Genesis 10:5 in the Revised English Bible, they left out the word *gentiles*, and they mention just the people of the coast and islands, who actually were the gentiles. However, a little later in Genesis 11:1, it says, "And the whole earth [which, as far as God was concerned was Asia Minor] was of one language, and of one speech."

This is contradictory to what was given earlier because they were all speaking after their own tongues (Genesis 10:20). They definitely did not speak one common language. They all spoke in their own tongues or languages, as mentioned over and over in Genesis 10.

In conclusion, all those people were not speaking the same language as implied. Most likely, the Lord worried about the progress the Egyptians had already made with their magnificent buildings and pyramids. Pyramids were in existence and being built in Egypt, on Malta, in Mexico, and in South America in Chile and Peru, just to name a few countries.

CHAPTER 11

The Tower of Babel

One Language versus Multiple Tongues

Genesis 11 begins with "And the whole earth was of one language and of one speech. Those people did not die in the flood? One language? Not according to the previous chapter. There everybody was talking in his own tongue, each one—Shem, Ham, and Japheth and their descendants, along with the Gentiles who had their own country and were speaking after their tongues, which is in their own language. So why all of a sudden was their one language? Strange! And not true!

"And it came to pass, as they journeyed from the east that they found a plain and they dwelt there." That must have been what was then called the whole earth.

Here we are confronted with the east again too. The east must have had a great significance, as it is mentioned many times, like "eastward in Eden." The following are some references to the east:

- The River Hiddekel goes toward the east of Assyria.
- He placed at the east of the garden a cherubim.
- It says, "And dwelt in the land of Nod, on the east of Eden."
- Sephar is mentioned as a mount of the east.
- It says, "As they journeyed from the east …"

Also, every altar in a Catholic Church is always oriented toward the east.

This is only six instances, but the *east* is mentioned about 127 more times in the Bible.

The Attempt to Build the Tower of Babel (Genesis 11)

"And they said: let us build us a city and a tower, whose top may reach into heaven, and let us make us a name, lest we be scattered on the face of the whole earth." How strange that they could anticipate what was going to happen!

Anyway, they obviously had no idea about all the technical difficulties they would have to overcome to build a tower of any size. They were not exactly civil engineers as we know them now. However, they were able to do amazing things back then already.

"And the Lord came down to see the city and the tower, which the children of men had built." He could not see all that from above? Like we humans say, "I have to see it with my own eyes." That amounts exactly to what God did. He had to come down and see it directly. The people had surmised, "Let us build a tower, which may reach into heaven."

"And the Lord said behold, the people are one, and have all one language and now nothing will be restrained from them, which they have imagined to do."

But according to the previous chapter, they were all speaking in their own tongues. So, what gives? To imagine is to picture something first in your mind, and then according to the Lord, nothing will be restrained from you, once you have imagined something in your mind.

Was God really afraid that those people could build such a structure to come unannounced and all of a sudden into heaven by means of a tower without dying? Originally, He saw what was going on from above. But now He had to come down. In the biblical days, the Gods came down quite often; later on and presently, that does not happen anymore. At least it is never mentioned and never observed.

Again, this is kind of early after the creation and the Gods did not know what to expect. They wanted to keep a close watch on the people. This was fairly easy, because there were not too many people around yet, at least in whom the Gods showed interest—that is, only in the offspring now from Noah. The Gods kept a close tab on their chosen people and cared less about the Gentiles, who also existed. Compare that to the more than six billion people now on earth.

When God created man, He also created them with imagination. Here God determines that by creating different languages, He can and will stop progress. And the Lord said to the other God or Gods, "Let us go down, and there confound their language, that they may not understand each other's speech. He did not like that the people were one. We realize the slogan: "United we stand; divided we fall" does not apply here in this instance.

God wanted the opposite. So, the Lord scattered them abroad on the face of all the earth, just as the people had already anticipated. God did not know what might happen. God sounds like He was getting worried.

Great! Can you imagine the Gods being worried about a tower being built all the way up to heaven—wherever that might be? Past the moon probably? That would be 238,000 miles high and still going and going. That would be unheard of and an impossible feat.

Now God got the other Gods involved. Genesis 11:7 says, "Let us go down, and there confound their language, so they cannot understand each other." In other words, then they will stop building the tower.

God is the instigator, and the other Gods followed suit. Now they are worried that the people were getting too smart for their own good. Building a tower was going too far for the Gods? Can you imagine if those people had exploded an experimental A-bomb or were in the process of cloning people or animals? Makes you wonder what would have happened then. Can you imagine the Gods coming down to Florida or Houston or Russia to shut down the space program? It is not even a threat to them now. And the Gods could care less.

Nowadays, the Gods, from all indications, don't care anymore about what is going on here on earth. It certainly looks that way. Is it because in the Old Testament, the Gods spent a lot of time on individuals and events like Cain, Noah and his ark, Moses and his people leaving Egypt, and so on?

Well, back to the Gods, who did not want a tower to be built. At least now, at the present time, as far as we know, the Gods don't notice and observe like they used to. It becomes obvious that the Gods in the relatively short period after creation wanted to keep a close tab on everything and every event going on down below.

As mentioned earlier, the first one to die was Abel. God said to Cain, "The voice of your brother's blood cried to me from the ground." At the present time, there must be a lot of blood crying to high heaven, probably constantly, but nobody is getting cursed.

It is impossible to keep track of everybody who dies at present, by human standards, and also pay attention to each and every one dying or living. In China, with the earthquake in 2008, more than seventy thousand people perished all in one swoop, and at approximately the same time, a cyclone in Myanmar wiped out close to one hundred thousand people. In the earthquake in Haiti, more than two hundred thousand people died.

Gods can do anything, we are told over and over. And we are supposed to accept that, but can we? The Gods have their limitations too; that's for sure!

In Matthew 10:30 and Luke 12:7, we are told, "But the very hairs of your head are all numbered." That means all your hair is there and accounted for. In other words, God has taken it upon Himself to keep track of each and every hair on every human being—accept, of course, when you are bald. Too bad they could not keep track of heart attacks, strokes, and cancers instead of missing a hair.

According to the *American Peoples Encyclopedia*, the first pyramids in Egypt were built in 3200 to 2780 BC.

The tower of Babel episode occurred in 2247 BC. This shows that the Egyptian pyramids were built close to a thousand years before the tower of Babel was started. God did not care what the Egyptians were doing, because they were not his chosen people. However, the Egyptians did build magnificent buildings and structures while the Israelites where still living in tents for almost a century. The encyclopedia states that the temple in Babel was built in the shape of a pyramid and so was the tower of Babel. Pyramids were also built in Mexico and South America—as a matter of fact, all over the world.

So, in the beginning, the Gods created the earth, but why is it that there have been found animals and human remains that were around not millions but hundreds of millions of years before the creation—if ever there was a creation?

Archeologists have shown that there were humans on earth who could not have been created by the Gods. They have found remains of human skeletons that were more than a hundred million years old.

In conclusion, all those people were not speaking the same language as implied. Most likely, God worried about the progress the Egyptians had made with their magnificent buildings and pyramids. Pyramids were in existence and being built in Egypt, on Malta, in Mexico, and in Chile and in Peru, just to name a few countries. So why were the Gods concerned about the tower? As far as the Gods are concerned, we can expect that a tower should not have been a threat to them. But alas, from all indications, it was.

CHAPTER 12

About Abraham and His Son

Abraham was not as great as he is made out to be by religion. When Abraham tried to mediate in God's plan to destroy Sodom and Gomorrah, he asked God, "Will you destroy the cities even if there are fifty good people in the city?" And the Lord said, "If there are fifty people, then I will spare the city." So, Abraham went from fifty to forty-five, then forty, then thirty, then twenty, and finally ten. Abraham stopped after God told him, "I will spare the city if there are only ten." Here Abraham showed that he wanted to plead for strangers.

God told Abram, as Abraham was called at the time, "Go to a land that I will show you and I will make of thee a great nation" and so on. There was a famine in the land, and Abram went down to Egypt. So, was Egypt the land He was going to show Abram? And when Abram got near to enter Egypt, he said to Sarai his wife, "You are pretty to look at, and when the Egyptians see you, then they will kill me, for your sake. So, say that you are my sister; that it may be well with me for your sake and I shall live because of you."

Nice going! He is trying to save his rear at Sarai's expense. He darn well knew what they were going to do with her. So, it happened. And the woman was taken into pharaoh's house for the purpose of him having sex with her.

Later, the pharaoh found out she was Abram's wife. He said, "Take your wife and get the heck out of here." And they sent him away, with his wife and all that he had.

You would think Abram would learn his lesson from this episode. No, sir, look what happened next.

In Genesis 20, we read, "And Abraham said of Sarah his wife, she is my sister, and Abimelech king of Gerar sent, and took his wife." Not to cook dinner or to make a drink for him. No, the only reason was again to have sex with her!

But God came to Abimelech in a dream and said to him, "Behold, thou art but a dead man, for the woman whom thou has taken; for she is a man's wife." Abimelech did not know that she was somebody else's wife; nevertheless, God told him, You are but a dead man." God was harassing the wrong man! God did not tell Abram, "Go and get your wife, and I will help you." No, sir. He had to threaten the wrong man.

Abimelech said, "Lord, did he not say unto me, she is my sister? And she, even she herself said, he is my brother." That poor king had no idea that she was Abraham's wife. Yet God was going to kill him if he did not return the woman.

So, Abraham did it again. Why did God not say to Abraham, "Don't even think about telling them your wife is your sister!" He had done it before! Abraham himself was responsible for his deeds! But he could not see it that way. And God did not intervene either, only when it had happened—as always, not when it was about to happen or when it was happening but only after it had happened, then He took action. This is typical God.

The bottom line was Abraham did not trust God to save him when needed.

Abimelech said to Abraham, "Why did you do this to me?"

And Abraham said, "Indeed, she is my sister; she is the daughter of my father, but not the daughter of my mother; and she became my wife."

He said to Sarah, "This is your kindness which you will show to me; at every place we shall come, say of me, he is my brother." Again, no trust in God!

Leviticus 18:9 tells us that God made a law, among some 600 others, that "you shall not uncover the nakedness of your sister, the daughter of your father, or mother, whether she is born at home or abroad, even so their nakedness you shall not uncover." This law came later, after Abraham sold his wife out to King Abimelech. Those laws were given to Moses.

So, Abraham skated this time, luckily for him. Nevertheless, he was trying to save himself at his wife's expense. Not much of a husband, and you would not be proud of a guy like that either.

"And it came to pass, that the Lord did tempt Abraham" (Genesis 22: 1). God likes to tempt. When Jesus taught everybody how to pray, he began, "Our father who is in heaven," and then He continued with "and lead us not into temptation"! This shows that even Jesus knew what the Lord was capable of.

He will tempt you when He sees fit!

But alas, He tempted Abraham to take his only son with Sarah to offer the boy up to him. When a God tempts, he definitely does not know what is going to happen beforehand and what the result is going to be. That's why He has to tempt, just to see what the outcome of the temptation will be.

Anyhow, Abraham left with the lad; I doubt that he informed Sarah about his plan to offer their son to the Lord. She probably would have *killed him* first before he could have taken off. She probably never would have said, "That's fine, honey. Go ahead and have fun doing it." So he went, and at the last minute, God intervened, luckily for him. Imagine him coming back home without him. Sarah would ask, "Where is Isaac?" and Abraham would casually say, "I offered him up to God." That would have been the end of them living together, or something worse might have happened to Abraham.

What kind of guy was Abraham? Twice while in Egypt, he almost lost his wife, by his own doing. Then he was going to kill his only son. Not much of a family man. However, he was not shy about asking God to save Sodom and Gomorrah. He would do that for strange people, but his own family came second.

However, God's favorite person was not even Abraham. As I said earlier, God's favorite people were Noah, Daniel, and Job (Ezekiel 14:14). God did not have the slightest idea about Abraham, if he was going to kill his son or not; that was why He had to tempt him. He wanted to see what was going to happen after He did the temptation. That was what the temptation was all about. If God knew everything beforehand, then He would not have had to test Abraham.

In the NIV Bible, they changed the word *temptation* to "test." This boils down to basically the same. If you have to take a test at school, the teacher does not know if you are going to pass or fail the test. That is why you have to take the test.

Genesis 22:12 says, "Abraham was at the last minute stopped and was told: 'lay not your hand upon the lad; for **now I know** that: you fear God seeing that you have not withheld your son, your only son from me" (emphasis added). Observe God says, "Now I know that you fear God," but before then, He obviously did not know if Abraham would go ahead and kill his son. That is why He said "now." *Now* is at the present time. He had to test or tempt Abraham to see what he would do. And then when it came to a climax, He said, "Aha! Now I know!" Earlier, He did not know.

However, Abraham did it all as He said, out of fear of God, because he was afraid of what would happen to him if he did not kill his son and not because he loved or even trusted God.

Now we know that the Gods and human beings don't know what the outcome is going to be beforehand when they plan to tempt or test. Only after the temptation He knows, just like human beings!

In Deuteronomy 6:16, the Lord says, "You shall not tempt the Lord your God, as you tempted him in Massah." This was a place in the desert, where they murmured, about no flesh to eat. So, God was tempted. However, James made the statement, "God cannot be tempted," as recorded in James 1:13.

James 1:2 says, "My brethren, count it all joy when you fall into divers temptations." Oh boy, oh boy, what a joy! Typical James again.

James 1:12 says, "Blessed is the man that endures temptation: for when he is tried, he shall receive the crown of life." Temptation by God or Satan? Because when man endures temptation, he receives the crown of glory, according to James.

But in James 1:13, he says, "Let no man say when he is tempted, I am tempted by God." Then by whom is he tempted if not by God? Is it Satan? Then if you endure Satan's temptations, you can still receive the crown of glory. James is contradicting himself here and not for the first time either. It becomes obvious that James does not know what he is talking about as usual—just like John when he said nobody has seen God. Observe that James said, "God never tempted any man." Now read the following:

Jesus, in the Lord's Prayer, tells us to pray, "And lead us not into temptation, but deliver us from evil" (Matthew 6:13). Jesus knows what God is capable of. And it becomes clear that if we have to ask God not to get us into temptation, then we can see that James was all wrong when he said God did not tempt any man. Besides that, it is shown in the following:

In Genesis 22:1, it says outright, "And it came to pass after these things, that God did tempt Abraham." Yes, the Lord did tempt Abraham for sure, as it is said above. And He also tempted Adam with the tree of knowledge of good and evil. And Adam also failed that temptation.

Here it is shown, and we have proof that God does not know before it happens what is going to happen! This shows God has His limits too and is not omnipotent as we make Him out to be.

There were a couple of weird incidents with Isaac, Abraham's son. In Genesis 26:7, we read that Isaac did the same thing his father Abraham had done. He was in the country by the name of Gerar, which still had, it seems, the same King Abimelech. "And the men of the place asked Isaac of his wife; and he said, she is my sister; for he feared to say, she is my wife; lest, said he, [that is Isaac speaking here], the men of the place should kill me for Rebekah," his wife, because she was pretty to look at. And it came to pass, when he had been there a long time, that Abimelech looked out a window and saw Isaac having sex with Rebekah, his "sister." In the meantime, the king *knew* Rebekah a long time also.

Abimelech called Isaac and said, "I know for sure she is your wife. Why did you say, 'She is my sister'?"

She was not his sister, so Isaac had lied. He said, "Because, lest I die of her." Like father like son! And Abimelech sent him away peacefully.

Now when Isaac was lying on his deathbed, he was going to give Esau, his oldest son, his blessing. Romans 9:12–13 says, "It was said to her, the elder shall serve the younger. As it is written, Jacob have I loved, but Esau have I hated." Again, a God who hates! He could have disliked Esau, but outright hate him? But it seems that God can do whatever He likes. He can tempt, hate, curse, and do more ungodly things if He wants to.

Rebekah had two sons, twins, Esau and Jacob. Now Rebekah told Jacob, "Hurry up, because your father is about to give his blessing to Esau." So Rebekah figured out how to deceive her husband. By means of unscrupulous and deceiving ways, she made Isaac fall for her scheme. But God had already foretold that Esau would be a servant to Jacob, as mentioned. Nevertheless, it was through a scheme not becoming of the all-powerful Lord. Strange that the Lord allows things to happen His way, through lying and deceit. We could expect that to happen by means of the devil but not from God. However, God has allowed stranger things to happen on occasion, particularly when He secretly likes the idea. Like that time when the Israelites told the king, who had defiled their sister, that if he and all his men would get circumcised, then they would be friends. And they did, but after a few days, those Israelites killed them all with the sword when they were all lying in pain. God permitted things like that. One can clearly see what would have happened if it was the other way.

CHAPTER 13

God, Moses, and the Pharaoh

How did it all come about? How did Moses get the Israelites to move out of Egypt?

God originally made a covenant with Abraham. "And I will give to you, Abraham, and to thy seed after thee, all the land of Canaan, for an everlasting possession" (Genesis 17:8). And Jacob dwelled in the land of Canaan, the Promised Land. And there was a famine in Canaan.

How nice of God to give to Abraham and his seed after him all the land of Canaan, but now they had to go out of this land because of a famine. God gave them the land, and then they had to leave the country, which was just given to them, making God more or less an Indian giver.

Joseph, who was one of Jacob's sons, had become the second in command in Egypt. He was the governor of Egypt. The pharaoh was the king of Egypt.

Genesis 45:17–18 says, "And the Pharaoh of Egypt said to Joseph: go into the land of Canaan, and take your father and your house holds, and come to me, and I will give you the good of the land of Egypt, and you shall eat the fat of the land."

What more could one want?

And all of them there were sixty-six, who went into Egypt. And it certainly did not take them all that long to come from

Canaan to Egypt, possibly a couple of weeks, a month at most. It took the Israelites *forty years* through the desert to go to Canaan from Egypt.

Genesis 46:3 says, "God spoke to Jacob: fear not to go to Egypt; for I will make of you a great nation." Again, a promise.

Genesis 48:21 says, "So the Israelites moved to a territory in Egypt, called Goshen. And Jacob said to Joseph: behold I die: but God shall be with you, and bring you again into the land of your fathers."

Jacob was right, however how long it would take and with a lot of tribulation to boot. However, Joseph died and everybody stayed in Goshen. So, Jacob was not correct in predicting the immediate future. And it seems God forgot all about Jacob's prediction. After the famine was over, they just stayed in Egypt, because they liked it there and never went back to the land of their fathers, which was Canaan.

In Isaiah 41:14, the Lord says, "Fear not, thou worm Jacob, and ye man of Israel." Strange that Jacob is called a worm. Joseph died and was embalmed and buried in Egypt. They were free to go out of Egypt anytime, but they just stayed, they acted as if it had become their land too. And they forgot all about Canaan—with dire consequences.

God did not tell the Israelites to go back to Canaan and out of Egypt, but as a God, He knew what would happen if they did not. He waited until it was too late, so He could show how great He was by doing the ten plagues, and then He bragged about it over and over. So, it could become a feast for the Israelites to celebrate the Exodus from Egypt.

Oh, well. So be it.

Let's examine the strange things that happened with Moses in pharaoh's time. When the Lord ordered Moses and the elders of Israel to go to the king of Egypt, Moses was supposed to say, "The Lord God of the Hebrews has met with us, and now let us go. We implore you, to give us three days in the wilderness, so we may sacrifice to the Lord our God" (Exodus 3:18).

Here, the Lord calls Himself "the Lord God of the Hebrews," not the God of Abraham, Jacob, and Isaac; not Jehovah or God Almighty, or even I Am That I am, because the Lord knew He had to let the pharaoh know that he was the God of the Hebrews— quite different than what Moses had to tell the Israelites. But the pharaoh would understand when he said the Hebrew God. All the other names would not have made sense to him.

"Give us three days." Oh, come on now. Don't believe that after three days they would have gone back from the wilderness to the pharaoh in Egypt, because then they would have been going on as planned away from Egypt. This was an outright plot and a lie. And this lie became more or less transparent even to the pharaoh at that time.

In Exodus 3:18–19, the Lord continues, "And I am sure that the Pharaoh will not let you go, no not by a mighty hand." In other words, not by a long shot. God knew that too. So, if God knows that the pharaoh won't let them go, what is the reason behind this?

God continues, "And I will stretch out my hand, and smite Egypt, with all my wonders [Isn't that wonderful?], I will do in the midst thereof: and after that he will let you go." So, God says here, "I first want to do my show of wonders [what a show], and then he will let you go." This is God's ego showing. He wants to show the ten plagues, just to show how great He is. This is brutal when you think about it, because it does not benefit anybody, except God's ego.

Now, in Deuteronomy 7:15, we read, "And the Lord will take away from thee all sickness, and will put none of the evil diseases of Egypt, which you know, upon thee." So here the Lord calls those plagues evil. In essence, He committed Himself to do evil.

Now we see what God wants to do. He first wants to give His performance of all His wonders, which are the ten plagues, also known as evils, see previous paragraphs. God wants to do His ten plagues, bringing misery to the Egyptian people and bringing the pharaoh to his knees.

One of the plagues include that they will lose their firstborn child. This is awful. This is our compassionate God? The children die just to make His point?

Well, we have seen before that He only cares about Israelites, and He certainly does not care much about Egyptians—only if they care and do something nice for the Israelites, which the Egyptians did many times. And He does not care much about babies or little children either, or for that matter, females. Even for animals, he has no compassion (see Exodus 34:7).

God wants Moses and the pharaoh to wait until all ten plagues (evils) have been done. This has nothing to do with the pharaoh, even though he will lose his firstborn too; it is about all the Egyptian people who will suffer. But we know God. He shows no compassion. He treated Job the same way, just to show His glory.

We did the same thing by bombing the German population; however, Hitler was the culprit. Was it because the German people were guilty by association?

And God continues, "After that he will let you go" (Exodus 3:20). After all those plagues (evils), then and only then, he'll let them go. "And the Lord said to Moses, see that you do all those wonders before the Pharaoh, which I have put in your hand." And now, here it comes.

God continues, "But I will harden his heart, that he shall not let the people go" (Exodus 4:21).

Here we have a typical case of setting somebody up! It is a pure setup. Even if the pharaoh wanted to let the people go, which he wanted to do several times, he could not, because God had taken control of his heart every time. So, there is no more free will! According to the dictionary, a *setup* is a contest or match arranged to result in an easy victory.

Exodus 7:13 says, "And he hardened Pharaoh's heart, so that he harkened [listened] not to Moses and Aaron, as the Lord had said."

Exodus 10:1–2 reads, "And the Lord said to Moses; 'go to the pharaoh, for I have hardened his heart, so that I can show my signs before him.'" This is the same as saying to Moses, "Go to the pharaoh, for I made it so that he no longer has a free will, so that I can show my signs before him."

The pharaoh cannot do whatever he thinks is right! He has no control over himself until all ten plagues (evils) have come about. He can't control himself anymore, because God has set him up.

And God continues, "That you may tell your son, and your son's son, what things I have done in Egypt."

It does not seem important enough to tell their daughters too, only their sons. And did you tell them also that God hardened the pharaoh's heart so the poor guy did not have a thing to say in the outcome? In other words, he was set up?

God did not say, "And to make all the Egyptian people miserable. Because I am a compassionate God."

Here follows some examples of the pharaoh's willingness to let the people go.

Exodus 8:8 says, "Then the Pharaoh called for Moses and Aaron, and said entreat the Lord that He takes the frogs away from me and my people, and I will let the people go, so they can sacrifice to the Lord." No, he did not let them go because God hardened his heart. Again, it was a setup.

Exodus 8:19 says, "The magicians of the Pharaoh said to him, this is the finger of God. Let them go. But Pharaoh's heart was hardened again."

Exodus 8:28 says, "And the pharaoh said: 'I will let you go, that you may sacrifice to the Lord your God in the wilderness." And then he envisioned them coming back? Same deal again, the pharaoh did not have a chance, because God did it to him again. But his initial intention was good.

Exodus 9:27–28 says, "And the pharaoh called for Moses and Aaron, and said I have sinned this time; the Lord is righteous, and I and my people are wicked, and I will let you go, and you shall stay no longer." It was to no avail, because God did harden his heart again.

Exodus 10:7–11 says,

> And pharaoh's servants said to him, let the men go, that they may serve the Lord their God, do you still not know that Egypt is destroyed? And the Pharaoh said to Moses and Aaron: Go: serve the Lord your God: but who are they that shall go? And Moses said everything and everyone will go. And he said to them let the Lord be so with you, as I will let you go, and your little ones. Go now you who are men, and serve the Lord, for that you did desire. And they were driven out from pharaoh's presence.

So far so good. This time, the pharaoh told them in no uncertain terms to go. The Lord did not even harden his heart in this episode. It was probably an oversight on the Lord's part, or He could not care less. Nevertheless, it appears that the pharaoh was sincere when he made this statement. But Moses and Aaron did not even take him up on it. Because they knew that God wanted all the plagues to be carried out first.

Here was an opening for them, and they could have taken him up on the offer to go. But that would not be according to God's plan. Because then all the plagues had not come about yet. Nevertheless, this time, God did not harden the pharaoh's heart even when he was willing to let them go. Now God continues with the plagues (the evil plagues) after the pharaoh told Moses to go. Now God did not harden his heart, and the pharaoh said go, but Moses did not take him up on it. So, an oversight of God?

Even in spite of the okay from the pharaoh to go, the Lord now said to Moses, "Stretch out your hand over the land of Egypt, so that the locust plague may come over the land of Egypt" (Exodus 10:13).

Exodus 10:16–17 says, "Then the Pharaoh called for Moses and Aaron in haste and he said, I have sinned against the Lord your God, and against you. Now therefore forgive I pray thee, my sin only this once and ask your Lord your God, that He may take from this death only."

But the Lord did it again; He hardened his heart again, so he would not let the Israelites go.

Exodus 10:24 says, "And there was darkness. And the Pharaoh called Moses, and said: Go ye, and serve the Lord." Again, the pharaoh wanted them to go, but the Lord hardened his heart again. "But the Lord hardened his heart and he would not let them go" (Exodus 10:27).

Here we have it many, many times that the pharaoh wanted them to go, but the Lord hardened his heart, so he could not let them go.

God had to have it His way as He had said already in the beginning. But from all indications, there was no need for God to continue the evil plagues. God wanted to finish his ten evil plagues regardless of all the suffering he caused to the people and all the animals. And somehow, He must have enjoyed doing all those evil things!

Isaiah 45:7 says, "I form the light and create darkness, I make peace and create evil: I the Lord do all those things." Here we have it, a God who does create evil, and He does it too whether you like it or not.

Now for the last plague, the firstborn was to be killed of all humans and animals alike in Egypt.

Exodus 11:4–5 says, "And Moses said, thus said the Lord, about midnight will I go into the midst of Egypt: and all the firstborn in the land of Egypt shall die, from the firstborn of Pharaoh, even unto the first-born of the maid servant who is behind the mill: and of all the first born of beasts."

Exodus 12:29 says, "The Lord killed all the first born human beings in the land of Egypt, and all the firstborn of not only cattle, but of all beasts."

Again, God shows no love for animals. What did those creatures have to do with the Israelites being held captive? Nothing at all! But God had to rub it in, it seems like. He did not care as almost always about animals.

Earlier, in Exodus 9:3, we read, "And the Lord brought about a cattle plague, murrain, which killed all the cattle in Egypt, which included horses, asses, camels, oxen, goats and sheep, but not one from the Israelite's cattle died." That was the end of all the Egyptian cattle or beasts. Here once more: "And all the cattle of Egypt died, which included all the horses." This is all written in Exodus 9:6.

Exodus 9:3, again, says, "The hand of the Lord is upon your cattle which are in the field, upon your horses, asses, camels, oxen and sheep. There shall be a very grievous murrain." This happens to be a deadly plague, a pestilence (*Standard Encyclopedic Dictionary*).

One of the next plagues was hail and lightning. The command had been given, "Gather thy cattle." However, they were already dead from the previous plague (Exodus 9:19).

Exodus 12:29 says, "And the last plague, every firstborn human and all the firstborn of cattle will die."

Which cattle is He talking about? They were all already dead! Because in Exodus 9:6, it was proclaimed, "And all the cattle of Egypt died." So no more cattle—or horses!

In Exodus 11:10, the last plague is described, making the feast for every Jew. It is called Passover. It is emphasized one more time: "And Moses and Aaron did all these wonders before the Pharaoh: and the Lord hardened Pharaoh's heart almost every time he wanted to let them go, so that he would not let the children of Israel go out of Egypt." God had to bring it up, one more time, that He hardened Pharaoh's heart.

Now, in Exodus 12:29, it says, "And it came to pass, that at midnight the Lord smote all the first born in Egypt; and all the first born of cattle." However, all the cattle were already dead. After that, the pharaoh let everybody go, and God did this time not harden his heart. So finally, they made their way to and through the Red sea.

Exodus 14:7 says, "And he, the pharaoh, took six hundred chosen chariots, and all the chariots of Egypt.

Exodus 14:9 continues, "But the Egyptians pursued after them, all the horses and chariots of the Pharaoh, and his horseman, and his Army."

How can that be? All the horses had died earlier during the murrain plague, remember? So where did all the horses come from to run the six hundred chariots and his horseman? Besides, in the last plague, all the firstborn horses died. So, this whole story about the pharaoh pursuing the Israelites and going into the parted sea, which Moses had parted for the Israelites, was a fable.

Now all the horses and chariot drivers drowned when the sea took its original form; that is farfetched. Because of all the men with their horses mounted in front of the chariots, they could not be there, because all the horses were dead. There was not a horse available for the chariots!

So, in conclusion, we can say that God failed to warn the Israelites to get out of Egypt when there was nothing holding them back. God made it impossible for the pharaoh to let them go, because He hardened his heart every time the pharaoh wanted them to leave and set him up so he would not let them go. God killed all the horses in the murrain plague, and consequently there were no horses available to go in hot pursuit after the Israelites.

There also is no mention of the Israelites doing a three-day sacrifice in the desert after they left Egypt. That would have been impressive if they had done it, but like I mentioned earlier, it was just a plot and a lie!

So, what does this story tell us? I leave it up to every individual to draw his or her own conclusions.

CHAPTER 14

The Pharaoh's Magicians and about Diverse Gods in History

I t is amazing how pharaoh's magicians could do some of the plagues originated by God. Those magicians could also make snakes out of sticks. In spite of Moses's snakes devouring the magicians' snakes, the magicians also did make snakes out of sticks. This was quite a feat by itself. And it was not done by tricks either (Exodus 7:12).

Now we don't know if the magicians' snakes could have also eaten the snakes from Moses, because they were gone, so it could not be reversed. Nevertheless, it was a feat that nobody has ever been able to duplicate since that time. A magician nowadays who can make snakes out of sticks would shock the whole world. From God, we could expect something like that, but of humans we don't. But those magicians did! Amazing.

Also, the magicians could turn water into blood, which happened to be the first plague (Exodus 7:22). They don't say what blood type it was. But it was the Lord's first plague and it must have colored the water red and did make it look like blood. However, it is puzzling that when all the water was turned into blood by Moses that there was any water at all available for the magicians to show that they also could turn water into blood. But somehow, they managed nevertheless.

Exodus 8:7 says they could also bring up frogs upon the land. This was the second plague. Pharaoh's magicians could do that too. This was quite a fantastic feat for those magicians!

Religion claims that it was Satan doing all that. But those men were magicians and they could do all those marvelous things. Besides, would God let Satan interfere with his grandiose scheme? The Egyptians were known to do great things besides building pyramids. Would God let Satan intervene directly in His plans?

No, God messed up Himself when He killed all the horses in the murrain plague. So, the pharaoh could never ride his chariots without horses, and he could never have pursued the Israelites through the desert and into the Red sea. And to top it all off, all the firstborn horses had also died.

Anyhow, after the first two plagues, the magicians could not keep up anymore with the next plague from God. So now they gave up and never even tried any of the next plagues. However, two out of the ten plagues were duplicated. Those magicians did not even know the God of Israel; they had their own Gods. Those Gods were respected and worshipped by them, as we can expect.

At the time of Joseph telling the pharaoh that God would show him the interpretation of his dreams, it appears the pharaoh took it that the Lord was like one of the Egyptian Gods, a different God altogether, or just a God the Hebrews worshipped. The God of Israel would not have anything to do with the Egyptians, except when they would help and assist the Israelites—like at the time of the exodus, when He only needed them to show how great He was by doing his "wonders."

Only when the Egyptians helped the Israelites were they good enough, like during the time of Joseph and at other times when they helped to defeat the enemies of the Israelites.

Joseph was not a missionary, and God did not need any help, only in the time of Jesus did missionaries come about.

This certainly would not have gone over to well with the Egyptians if they had tried to convert the pharaoh. Joseph, for one, never told the Egyptians, according to the records, that his God was the only God, and neither did Jacob earlier when he met the pharaoh. One just does not do that, when one is a guest.

During Hurricane Katrina, on the news, two preachers were being interviewed. And they were asked, "What are you still doing here?" They answered, "We are here to help God."

God was the one who brought the hurricane about and set everything into motion. So how could they help God if He was the one who caused all the disaster and the evil in the first place? Did God need help with that or anything else? So, it made them accomplices.

The bottom line is God did not want anything to do with people who were not circumcised. This was the covenant He made with the Israelites, besides quite a few other covenants He made with them.

CHAPTER 15

Seeing God

N obody has seen God, so we are told. Even John made the statement in John.1:18, "No man has seen God at any time." Too bad he said that, because we can prove that he did not know what he was talking about!

Jesus Himself said, "Who has seen me has seen God." Where was John coming from when Jesus Himself contradicts his statement?

Adam and his helpmeet certainly did see the Gods, while still in the Garden of Eden, unless they were like John said "no man." God was looking for Adam to have a conversation with him. They both had discussions with God. God even called to Adam in the garden because He could not find him. In other words, God was looking for Adam so He could talk to him.

Jacob and Moses saw and talked to God, face-to-face.

Exodus 24:9–10 says, "Then went up Moses and Nadab and Abihu, and seventy of the elders of Israel and they saw the God of Israel!" Seventy-three people saw not only the glory of God but also the God of Israel!

Notice it said "the God of Israel." He was not a God of other people or countries. No, He was specifically the God of Israel! It sure looks like God did not want to be a God of anybody but the Israelites. Nevertheless, they all saw him.

Exodus 24:11 continues, "And upon the nobles of the children of Israel He laid not His hand; they also saw God [in spite of what John said] and they saw God and did eat and drink." Again, a substantial number of people saw God there and seemingly enjoyed themselves.

Genesis 32:30 says, "And Jacob called the name of the place Peniel: for I have seen God face to face."

In Deuteronomy 34:10, we read, "And there arose not a prophet since in Israel like unto Moses, whom the Lord knew face to face."

Now we have enough proof that there were many people who saw the Lord, in spite of John proclaiming that nobody has seen God at any time.

In Exodus 33:11, a different God came about who changed everything in midstream. Now the God is the Lord! So, the Lord changed His mind after He showed himself to multiple people; He changed everything. Well, we can say it is His prerogative.

Here is the Lord talking again. After Moses said to the Lord, "I beseech thee show me your glory" (Genesis 13:18).

Exodus 33:20 says, "And the Lord said: 'you cannot see my face for there shall no man see me, and live.'" So, God's face is God's glory? What is this? Certainly, this must be another God talking, for sure. Otherwise, He appears to be capricious!

In Exodus 33:22, the Lord continues, "And it shall come to pass, while my glory passes by that I'll put you in a cliff of the rock and will cover you with my hand while I pass by. And I will take away mine hand and you shall see my hind parts, but my face and front shall not be seen." This indicates God showed Moses his hind parts. So, Moses could not see his face, which Moses had asked for, but now Moses could only see his rear parts? Moses asked, "Show me your glory," and was told, "You cannot see my face only my rear end."

Something to look forward to. This must be a different God, and I will bring it up again that Adam, his wife, Cain, Jacob, and Moses did see God. And Jesus said, "If you have seen me, then you have seen God." Plus, seventy-two men and the nobles saw God and they ate and drank with Him!

Moses was fortunate he could speak to him face-to-face as a friend in Exodus 33:11. Makes one wonder if the Lord wore anything. Obviously, He did not; otherwise, it would not make any sense to show your rear. Big deal. Why did He do this? As a "favor" to Moses? In other words, Moses was being mooned by God, as this term is used in our vernacular and folklore here in the United States.

Was God naked? Yes. Otherwise, He would not have held his hand for Moses eyes. So, he could not see any more than the Lord allowed him to see. The Lord would rather show His hind parts than his face to Moses. Why did He only show his back parts to Moses when he could see his face when he was speaking to him earlier face-to-face. It probably was God! This is the Lord he was seeing now "face to rear," and it was the Lord.

Michelangelo, when he painted the ceiling of the Sistine Chapel, also painted God, showing God bending over with his pants down for everybody to see there. But this is not according to the Bible. Michelangelo probably got the idea that God was wearing some type of clothing and being in a bent over position most likely to moon the pope, whom he despised for having him paint the chapel instead of making statues, his favorite profession. And now the pope, when officiating, had to look at this scene from where he was sitting down below.

What is the point here? You will die if you see God?

This is everybody. Nobody sees God anymore. You would die anyway. Only after you die then maybe you can see Him. But nobody is looking forward to that—dying, that is.

Thus, now He becomes a phantom God, illusive, a specter, and a nonentity because the almighty Lord won't show Himself, He decreed! That's why we never hear or see Him anymore after God's statement, "Nobody will see me and live."

Clergy and parents make us believe He is still around even if over the ages there has been nothing but misery in this world.

Let's put it this way; is there any proof that God exists? How could He ignore all those millions of Jews murdered in concentration camps? Besides all the millions of non-Jews from all over Europe, including lots of gypsies. All this occurred in spite of the fact that the Jews are his chosen people, no less, with whom He made all kinds of pacts and covenants!

Deuteronomy 4:31 says, "For the Lord thy God is a merciful God. He will not forsake thee. Neither destroys thee, nor forgets the covenant of thy fathers, which He swore to them!" Only with the Jews did He make covenants. Did God forget the covenant of their fathers when the Jews needed Him most?

Deuteronomy 7:15 states, "And the Lord will take away from thee all sickness. [Look in Israel now, and you will see cancers, heart attacks, diabetes, and all kind of sicknesses.] And I will put none of the evil diseases of Egypt, which you know, upon thee. But I know plenty other diseases. [He admits they were evil, those diseases in Egypt], but I will lay them upon all that hate thee."

Most of the Nazis did hate the Jews, we all know, but did God put those evil diseases on the Nazis? Heck no, but the Jews needed help—did they ever! But the Jews were on their own all throughout that time. The Lord acted like his nose was bleeding. We know all those Jews prayed long and hard for help, particularly when death was staring in their faces all the time. But did He help them or listen to them? Heck no. He did let them all suffer and die. Maybe He did listen but did not want to hear them. Why? Who knows? That's why He is God. That's why religion likes to call Him mysterious.

Some of the Jews were lucky and escaped from or did not go to concentration camps for whatever reason. But the Gods did not control that obviously.

He loved the world so much and had so much compassion for everybody that He let millions of them die? He even offered up his only begotten son to die, temporarily, because He loved the world so much. Even if it was just for *a short time only* He gave up His son! He did not intervene with Hitler either. So, the omnipotent God did not lift a finger, like there is no God anymore, only silence.

This was not the only time in history; we only have to look at the Crusades, the Catholic Inquisition during the Middle Ages, and all through history the countless religious wars.

In World War II, German mothers, wives, brothers, and sisters prayed just as hard for their German soldiers as the American mothers, wives, brothers, and sisters prayed for their American soldiers, while they killed each other when they had a chance! And when the husbands or sons came back, they said, "Oh thank God." But just because they prayed that does not mean their prayers were heard or even listened to; those were just the lucky ones who returned in spite of the hundreds of thousands of soldiers on both sides who died and were prayed for.

In World War II, the Allies bombed whole cities to the ground in Germany, where there were no military targets just civilians. The cities—Leipzig, Dresden, Aachen, Cologne, and Berlin, to name a few—were bombed flat by the United States and Britain, which killed an estimated 600,000 civilians.

Fire bombings and atomic blasts killed up to 500,000 Japanese civilians who lived in Tokyo, Hiroshima, and Nagasaki (*Wikipedia*).

All those people prayed and begged God for their lives when engulfed in flames, particularly when they heard those whistling bombs coming down and explosion after explosion. *Is the next one going to hit our house? Oh, God, please help.* It happened, very rarely, that when the bombs stopped whistling, there would be no explosion, just a dud. Some duds came down where they would not have done any harm, like in a field or on an empty house or building. However, some duds did fall on houses, which were occupied.

As noted earlier, it seems from all indications God does not know or does not want to know what is going on in real time, when it is going on. Only after it has happened does He know, from all indications throughout the Bible.

As a boy, I always wondered how God could let his own houses (churches, cathedrals, temples, and synagogues) be bombed and sometimes destroyed completely.

If in need, it is human nature to call upon God, just like a security blanket.

How many times are prayers said for dying people! Then it is said when they die, "He needed him or her anyway, so He can hold him or her in His arms." Let's face it. He would not have arms enough to hold all the good people who are constantly dying all over the world.

People are so conditioned to praying that they don't realize it is their mind controlling most everything, including sickness!

Jesus said in Matthew 17:20, "Nothing shall be impossible to you" to the extent if you had faith like a mustard seed, you could move a mountain and do greater things than He did. Nobody has moved a mountain yet, and for what purpose would one move a mountain? And He did not say by praying, so most likely it must be by mind power.

People trust in metaphors. People even pray for popes, when they have died. When they die, then it's over, either way, according to religion; they go to heaven or to hell. No praying will get them out of hell. Now please tell me why do popes need praying for when they are dead? They are human beings, and they can and do sin? Is that why they are prayed for? It makes one wonder.

Let's face it, what happened in New York on September 11 is nothing compared to what happened in World War II, except that it happened in the United States. Nevertheless, it was and still is a terrible event, particularly when so many lives were lost (about six thousand). Except for the Civil War, we have always fought wars on foreign soil, and we still do. So, we are not used to fatalities in our country.

In World War II, ten, twenty, fifty, and even thousands of people died when the B-17s or B-24s or other bombers dropped all their bombs on cities.

God does not seem to care who is fighting whom. If there is proof at all that there still is a God, how about September 11?

The strange thing is that after the war, the countries we fought, Japan and Germany, became some of our best allies. And boy oh boy did a lot of prayers go up on both sides during that war. But could God take sides? It seems only during most of the wars Israel fought in biblical times did He take a side. At present time, every country that wants to fight has to be prepared for thousands of casualties. Also, anybody who gets a fatal bullet has to die, regardless if the person is prayed for or not.

There is a saying, "Seeing is believing." However, we don't see God anymore, so how can we believe?

CHAPTER 16

The Foreign Gods Who Have Existed throughout History

History tells us one of the most famous Gods was Zeus, and he was the highest God of ancient Greece, Rome, and surrounding countries. Homer called him the father of Gods and men. In Rome, they called him Jupiter. People really believed in him. For them, he was the only existing God, just like all the Christians go for the Jewish God.

Another great and famous God was Apollo. He was known and honored all over western Asia and surrounding areas.

If it had not been for Jesus, the Gods in the Old Testament would only be known at present to the Jews. Please think about that statement. What if you were not a Hebrew or nowadays a Jew? Who would want a God who only takes care of, protects, and helps Jewish people—and still will, according to Revelations. Not much of an incentive there.

Allah is also a very powerful God all over the world to the Muslims. The religion of Islam requires belief in only one God, and that is Allah.

In the Scandinavian countries, Iceland, and some other countries. they worshipped Wodan. In England, he was known as Odin. Then there was Thor, the God of thunder. Our weekdays are named after these Norse Gods, except Saturday, which is named after Saturn; Sunday, which is named after the sun; and Monday, which is named after the moon! Tuesday is named for the deity Tiw, a Teutonic God. Wednesday is named after the Scandinavian God Wodan. Thursday is named after the God of thunder, which was Thor. And Friday was named after the Goddess Freya. So here we have a whole week named after strange Gods and objects. In those days, people really believed in those Gods, just as much as people now believe in Jesus.

The people in the Scandinavian countries were fierce and were great warriors. It seems fighting was all they did for a living. There was a special heaven for the warriors, called walhalla, where they could go only if they died in war! If you died let's say from sickness but were a warrior, then you went to another heaven, which was inferior to walhalla. People who died of old age or for other reasons, as long as it was not in battle, would also go to walhalla but as servants to the fallen fighters. And virgins were readily available to the warriors. When the fighters were killed in battle, they would go straight to heaven and be received with open arms, so they claimed. However, there was never a reference to hell!

Around AD 1100, when the crusaders were going on crusades, the pope would give them blessings and tell them to kill as many of those heathens, who were of the Islamic faith, as they could, and if they died, they would go straight to heaven. So, the pope gave out free passes to heaven. Like the saying goes, "You can't take it with you when you die." But they had something to look forward to when they were in battle and staring death in the face.

When I was a teenager, I hitchhiked through France, and one night, I slept in an abandoned farmhouse. There was a small, old Bible lying on the kitchen table. In it, I found a little card, which said that the bearer of this card had free entry to heaven. That poor farmer left it behind and probably paid a good price for it. Now I carried that card a long time on me until you could not read it anymore. And I used it to brag about my free entrée to heaven. Alas, the Catholic Church got the money from the farmer. And who knows how many more they issued for a donation?

In India, they have quite a few Gods, and they still worship them, even up to the present day. So do the American Indians, the Aztecs, the Aborigines in Australia, the natives of Indonesia, the Indians of Peru, the Japanese, the Chinese, and more peoples, and they all live happily on and on. They don't worry about the Christian or Jewish Gods, yet they all live the same way we do with no adverse effects.

Now Jesus was one of the latest Gods, who came about, and there is quite a bit of data about Him available to show He is real. He makes a lot more sense than the Gods—even if the Jews don't recognize Him. The Jews, however, do believe in their Gods.

From all indications, during World War II, the persecutions of the Jews was caused by the Jews not believing in Jesus, according to Christian beliefs. So according to the Christians, the Jews had it coming. Even the Vatican was of that opinion. Because somebody in Israel at the time of Jesus's crucifixion supposedly said, "His blood come over us and our children."

How many religions do we need? Which is the right one?

When I was living in Los Angeles in the fifties, I counted in the *Los Angeles Sunday Times* the different Christian denominations listed and came to a grand total of seventy-one. Seventy-one different Christian denominations! All those denominations cannot agree on what is right in spite of all of them believing in the same God.

Amazing is it not? They all believe in the same God but have different dogmas and teachings about what is right and what is not. Each group believes they have the right religion for salvation and all the other religions are wrong! They are all going to anywhere but heaven because they don't do what they think is the right thing, as far as their religion is concerned.

As I have said before, churches are big business. How sad.

As an example, the following headline appeared in the *Las Vegas Review Journal* on September 12, 2009. "Christian Money Guru Gets Rich Mixing Faith, Funds."

At its core, the ninety-minute show was a millionaire preaching to a struggling flock and raised anew the question of whether his hugely profitable business—which he describes as a ministry—fits with Jesus's teachings. One person who subscribed to his ministry said, "It's not a ministry; to me it's an insult to the word.

The preacher does not deny mixing religion and business, and he doesn't apologize for getting rich doing it. He charges $5,100 for a three-day seminar. He is building a huge home on a $1 million lot in a gated community.

The Associated Press shows that he owns property worth more than $7 million, and he says that's low by a few million.

So here is an example of big business for church purposes. Well, good for him. It's great that he can do it. But it still proves that churches can be and are big business.

In the twelfth century, there was a bishop by the name of St. Malachi who came up with some pretty interesting predictions. He predicted that there would be a total of 111 popes. Well, he was wrong, because so far we have had at least 160 popes. And he said the end of the pope's empire was coming in the year 2021. He also predicted that the second-to-last pope would be Benedict XVI. One more pope would be installed after him with the name Petrus. And then it would be the end of the popes and supposedly the world.

CHAPTER 17

The Story of Job

I n Job 1:6, we hear, for the first time, Satan's name come up. Satan is also known as the Devil. Just like the Gods, he is known under different names, including Beelzebub, Demon, Devil, Lucifer, Lord of Flies, and so on (Lord of Flies comes from the New Testament).

Who is Satan? We can deduce that he was one of God's sons, albeit a fallen one.

Job 1:6 says, "Because, when the sons of God came to present themselves, before the Lord, then Satan was among the sons of God." So, he considered himself still one of God's sons. And He did crash the presentation ceremony. But what did God do? Did He call security and tell the guards to throw the bum out? To the contrary, God started a friendly dialogue with Satan, his supposed archenemy. If he is God's adversary, then God does not behave or act as if he is. No, God started a businesslike dialogue with Satan, and God asked Satan, "Where are you coming from?" In other words, "What are you doing here?" He had to ask again, because the all-knowing God did not know where Satan was coming from.

And Satan answered, "From going to and from on the earth and from walking up and down in it." Magma temperatures inside the earth are in the 1100 to 2100 degree F range (*American Peoples Encyclopedia*). If that is his domain, then that could be hell.

Quite a few people are of the opinion that hell is right here on earth anyway, considering how we have to suffer and have to go through all kinds of turmoil and misery here on earth, I can see how we are going through hell, right here, right now—like losing loved ones through tornados, hurricanes, earthquakes, floods, fires, droughts, car or plane crashes, or sea and space calamities and other types of accidents. We lose babies, infants, children, spouses, and parents.

Something here is amiss, very illogical. If God rewards you for doing things His way, then you go to heaven. Would it not be more logical then, if you don't do God's will, that God would be the one who sent you to hell? Does this mean then that Satan is working for God? Well, he has the job of supposedly sending people to hell. This does not make much sense either unless it is God who wants him to do that.

Why would the devil, if you do his bidding, send you to hell? In hell, one supposedly goes to a place where fire goes on for eternity, but you don't burn to death either. Your body stays here on earth, no matter how you die—in a fire, at sea, or blown to little pieces in an explosion—and then it is eaten up by scavengers, buried in a grave and eaten up by worms and all kinds of insects, or turned to ash by cremation.

No, it is the soul which supposedly goes to heaven or hell. In heaven, all you do is sing, "Hallelujah!" and yell, "Praise God!" all the time for eternity, because souls don't need to drink or eat or even sleep.

It's preposterous if you think about it.

If there is a Satan, then he knows darn well if you fall for him, you should know that there is something in it for you too. Not going to hell. Why would the devil reward you by sending you to hell, unless Satan made some secret kind of pact with God?

Where is hell anyway? When God created heaven and earth, there is no reference to the creation of hell too. So where did hell get its existence? Did Satan get some real estate from heaven to put hell in? As mentioned earlier, in one of the parables of Jesus, heaven and hell are side by side (Luke 16:23).

When God created heaven and earth, it does not say that He created hell.

Religion makes you believe that you either go to hell if you do not do God's will or you go to heaven if you do.

Well, Satan does not exactly carry a passport to come into heaven either, as you can see in Job 1:6. Satan has free access to and in heaven, and God and his angels don't stop him from going where he wants to go. He just shows up when he feels like it. From all indications, Satan walks freely around in heaven. As proof, I mentioned earlier Revelation 12:7. We are so conditioned to believe that hell and Satan are synonymous, and most Christian people have an inherited fear if they even hear the word *Satan* or *hell* mentioned.

Religion loves to put fear in everybody and makes everybody feel guilty.

Everybody is scared to no end, so they will do whatever the church wants them to do. Or else they are doomed. Now we know the church can and will control people through fear and guilt!

In the Old Testament, hell is never associated with Satan. In Hebrew, hell is called *shoal*, and it means "the grave." That's why hell is referenced as being down or down under.

We continue now with God and Satan. So, the Lord and Satan continue their dialogue, and it looks like they are going to make some kind of bet. God certainly was not antagonistic toward Satan, as we would expect.

God continues by asking again, "Where are you coming from?" He had no idea, it seems. He then asks, "Have you observed my man, Job? There is nobody like him on the whole earth."

"Sure," says Satan. "Does he fear You for nothing? He loves You because You give him everything he wants, but take it away from him, and he will curse You to Your face."

God falls for that argument. "And the Lord said to Satan. Behold everything he has is in your power. Only you can't kill him" (Job 1:12). In other words, "do what you want to him." What? He let Satan do what he pleased.

What a deal Satan got, and God does not seem to care what Job has to go through. Where is His compassion for the man? God brags about him but shows no mercy.

God is only interested in proving His point—just like He was with the pharaoh. Never mind Job. And Satan went from the presence of the Lord. He did not even say, "Okay, we got a deal." No, they understood each other perfectly.

What a deal they made. Now Satan could and would wipe out everything Job possessed.

Then it happened. A servant came to Job and let him know he lost most of his cattle; then he was told by another servant he had lost the rest of his cattle. Next, another servant came and told Job he lost all his camels and his servants. Next, he was told the fire from God had fallen from heaven and had burned all the sheep and his servants. And to top it off, he had yet another servant telling him that a great wind came and dropped the house on all his sons and his daughters, and it killed all ten of them—his seven sons and three daughters. He was told everything had happened in less than half an hour or maybe at the most ten minutes.

So, Satan got busy right away. He did not lose any time.

God knew darn well beforehand that He could win and make it so the outcome would be in His favor. He is supposed to be a God. So this bet was rigged. Satan should have known too that he was going to be the loser. But he was obviously counting on knowing how Job, or any man for that matter, would behave if confronted with circumstances like the ones Job just got into. But how about poor old Job? The gracious and loving God made Job go through hell by first having all his belongings destroyed—7,000 sheep, 3,000 camels, 500 pairs of oxen, and 500 female donkeys. This shows again God does not have much mercy for animals. A total of 8,500 animals, in one swoop, were wiped out. He certainly did not care much about what He had created—just dumb animals who could in no way give Him any glory. God gave His fiat to Satan to destroy all those animals and Job's kids also!

Job 1:16 says, "And the fire of God is fallen from heaven, and burned all the sheep and his very great household of servants." Did God help Satan and got involved by giving Satan His "fire"? "And the fire of God is fallen!"

And then to top it off, he had all his children killed, ten in all—seven boys and three girls. All this happened in less than an hour. This indicates that Satan can kill people too. At least he had permission from God to do that to Job's kids and all his servants.

Actually, Job got the bad news in less than ten minutes. One servant after the other came to Job. While one was still speaking, the next one showed up.

The merciful God gave Satan permission to do all that—not exactly indicative of a loving and kind God. He did it just to make his own point to Satan. He does not care much about Job. He lets him suffer, just to win the wager with Satan. He behaves again more like a mischievous human being than like a God.

"In its entirety, Job sinned not and did not charge God foolishly" (Job 1:22).

We can say now God had His way, so it's over, no more suffering by Job. Yeah, right! But is it?

For the second time, God makes a wager with Satan.

"Again, the sons of God came [for the second time] to present themselves to God and Satan came also to present himself again to the Lord" (Job.2:1–6). It seems one of God's sons, obviously Satan, failed Him somehow, but we can see that God still considers Satan one of His sons. He was His son and consequently stays His son.

Again, God starts a dialogue with Satan. God asks again, "Where are you coming from?" and Satan answers the same as the first time. God is asking questions because He does not know?

"And the Lord said again: have you observed my servant, Job? There is none like him on the whole earth. An upright man that fears God and shuns evil?" And now He starts to complain, as follows: "He said: although you [Satan] moved me against him [Job], to destroy him without cause" (Job 2:3).

Here, God laments over the situation, and He realizes what He has done to Job. But it's too late; He's already done it. God admits to Satan, "You are the one who moved me against Job." He also recognizes what went wrong!

Satan had gotten God's goat.

Now Satan starts again and says to God, "Job is still yours, because he lost all his possessions, but that is nothing, because all that a man possesses, he will give for his life. Now put forth Your hand and touch his bones and his flesh, then he will curse You to Your face." God had given Satan permission the first time to do anything to Job except kill him.

God falls for that second argument again, just like the first time, instead of saying, "Don't start again, boy. Enough is enough. I made my point. Now get out of here, because you have seen that he surely still loves Me. This was for real and true. And besides that, I won!" This shows God is not much of a businessman. God was holding all the cards, and all He had to do was to tell Satan to get lost and out of His sight. But He did not!

No, God takes him up again on that argument. He lets Satan do it again! And in essence, it's God and Satan against Job, just to satisfy God's ego again. God realized that Satan had moved against Him so Satan could destroy Job without cause. God said that to Satan.

What kind of God does not realize He has been had? He could not keep His own house in order.

"And the Lord said to Satan, behold, he is in your hand; but save his life."

How nice. So, what the Lord said was "I will make him sick for you. But you can't kill him." In other words, you can do what you want with him (Job 1:12), just like the first time. How nice and considerate.

What a deal Satan got, and the Lord does not seem to care what He does to Job. Where is His compassion for the man? God brags about him but shows no mercy toward him. Here, we have a similarity with Moses and the pharaoh. And here the Lord wants the same deal as with the pharaoh. At the end, He wants to show "how great I am."

It seems God has nothing against Satan. He was His son and stays His son. So, He makes a bet again, figuratively speaking, of course. When Jesus was in the desert and the devil tempted Him several times, Jesus did not fall for it. His son did not fall for Satan's tricks, but God does. And the consequences would have been tremendous for God if He had lost. Then it would not even have been in the Bible. That could never have happened. Then Satan would have had the upper hand.

Satan should have known he could never win against God, but he was convinced that Job, a human being, could not stand the torture for long. So God gave Satan the fiat to go ahead, and God made Job sick! Sickness compliments of the loving and caring God. Because Satan said to God, "Put forth Your hand and touch his bones and his flesh, then he will curse You." God did make Job sick; Satan did not.

"So went Satan forth from the presence of the Lord, and Job was smitten with sore boils from the sole of his feet unto his crown" (Job 2:7).

Job 2:10 says, "And Job said: shall we receive good at the hand of God, and shall we not receive evil, from God?" Job is well aware of God being capable of creating and doing evil. And that is exactly what God did; it was evil!

In Isaiah 45:7, God Himself says, "I form the light, and create darkness; I make peace, and I create evil, I the Lord do all those things." How about that? Our God creates evil, whether we like it or not, so we cannot blame everything evil that happens on Satan, regardless of Satan supposedly being the cause of some or most of the evil going around. So, if something goes drastically wrong with you, then accept it, because God can do evil things too. It's not necessarily Satan.

So poor Job, this guy was the sacrificial lamb who had to endure all this misery, like boils and other sickness, just so God could prove His point. Finally, God made it, and Satan thereby lost. What did God accomplish with all this? Only that He could say, "See I told you so." And God knew Job would persevere all through his tribulations. But Job had to go through hell all that time.

Can you imagine how sick Job was? Even one boil can drive you up the wall. He had his whole body covered with them, from head to toe. Yet he had conversations with his friends and he talked a lot all through his predicament. If you are that sick, then you certainly don't feel much like talking. Still, for forty-two chapters, he talked and he talked and he listened to God and to his friends and he talked some more. And he did do some cursing, not to God, but about being born, and he wished that he would die (Job 3 and Job 6:9). Let's face it, if you, the reader, do not know how it feels to have just one boil, then you have no idea how it was for Job, being all covered with them. You absolutely don't feel like talking! Because you are really sick and have pain and feel miserable;

Anyhow, he made it through the awful situation he was in, and God gave him as a reward two times more than he used to have as far as it goes for his animals. And again, he got seven sons and three more daughters. But it is hard to believe that he did not grieve the first ten kids he had, because it is human nature that he would sorely miss them. He did think about them, and he had all the memories of them. So, God did patronize Job and gave him twice as much as he had before for good behavior.

CHAPTER 18

The Gods Do a Lot of Things That Human Beings Would Do

From observation throughout the Bible, it becomes apparent that the Gods do show some ungodly behavior and they do behave more like human beings than Gods. Or is it the other way around? Do humans behave like Gods?

As mentioned in chapter 1, God says, "I am a jealous God." Human beings are quite often jealous too. If they want what other human beings possess, then jealousy comes about. Gods are not supposed to be jealous, because they can have everything they want. Jealousy is definitely not much of a godly trait. Jealousy is being intolerant of rivalry or begrudging another's possessions and accomplishments.

It is not so much what God is jealous about; the point is He *is* jealous! Why is God jealous? Is it because He can't control Himself, or is He similar to a human being?

God hates too. Romans 9:13 says, "Jacob have I loved, but Esau have I hated." Zechariah 8:17 says, "For these are things that I hate." Malachi 1:3 says, "And I hated Esau." And Ecclesiastes 3:8, "There is a time to love and a time to hate." Does this mean there is a time to love and a time to hate Satan? Jesus himself said, "Love thy enemies." If Satan is our enemy, then we should love him.

So, here we have a God who outright hates. This is what we don't expect from a God. But we know humans do hate.

Repent. To repent means: to feel remorse or regret, as for something one has done or failed to do, caused by a sense of guilt.

"And it repented, or regretted, the Lord that He had made man on earth (Genesis 6:6). In other words, He was sorry that He had created him. So, He was definitely not proud of or happy about the situation! Was it because things did not work out as expected? Another human trait! Feeling sorry about what you have done. Well, He did not have any idea it was going to work out the way it did.

"And the Lord repented of the evil, which He thought to do unto his people" (Exodus 32:14). Again, He was sorry to have just the thought alone and repented.

In 2 Samuel 24:16, it says, "For it repented the Lord." Judges 3:1 says, "And when the angel stretched out his hand upon Jerusalem to destroy it; the lord repented him, and said to the angel, it is enough." And in 1 Samuel 15:35, we read, "And the Lord repented that He had made Saul king of Israel." He was sorry about that too? Here it shows that the all-knowing, omniscient God did again not know beforehand what was going to happen to His chosen and appointed king.

Religious leaders like to say God knows everything, just like St. Nick. But it shows here that God had no idea after He anointed Saul how he would turn out. He does not know what is going to happen until it has happened! He cannot anticipate or foresee beforehand the outcome of what He does.

Religious leaders like to say it is all due to free will. Free will is only mentioned in the Bible in reference to the following:

1) burned offerings—Leviticus 22:18: "That will offer his oblation for all his vows, and for all his free will offerings, which they will offer to the Lord for a burnt offering. But the offering cannot have any blemish and must be perfect."

2) in some instances to gold and silver being offered to God (Ezra.8:28)
3) Psalm 119:108: "the free will offerings of my mouth."

These three mentions are all about free will and they relate to sacrifices and not according to the free will everybody is supposed to have. In other words, God does not have control over free will as religion tells us—only when it is His will. Remember what He did to the pharaoh to keep him under control to do His will. And the pharaoh did not have any free will at that time. So, it just does not exist, except in an irrelevant way. The pharaoh in Moses's time did not have free will because it was taken from him by God.

So, God was disappointed and He felt sorry that He had made Saul king over Israel. We like to believe at all times that Gods know, before they do certain things, what the outcome is going to be. But they just don't.

"The Lord repented for this: it shall not be, said the Lord" (Amos.7:3).

"The Lord repented for this: And again, this also shall not be, said the Lord God" (Amos 7:6).

Jonah 3:10 says, "And God repented of the evil, that He had said that He would do to them and He did it not." God was planning on doing evil. Just the idea of God doing evil is repulsive! God doing evil? We know He does. This we expect from Satan or human beings, not from God, regardless of the reason. Everybody knows evil is unacceptable and terrible, particularly if it is done by God. Otherwise, He is a God who is capable of doing evil. And He does, according to Isaiah 45:7. Here God Himself says, "I form the light, and create darkness, I make peace and I create evil, I the Lord do all these things!" So, He is even boasting about doing evil. Now if we analyze this text, then we can see if He did not create light, then there would be darkness. So, He did not have to create darkness! Darkness was there all along, when there was no light. In the same line, we can also say, if He did not create evil, then there would always be peace and that would be marvelous.

But alas, He made the decision to create evil. And Job said, "Shall we receive good at the hand of God, and shall we not receive evil?" From this we can learn that God is not all that nice, as everybody makes Him out to be. Au contraire.

Genesis 3:5 says, "And the serpent said to the woman in the Garden of Eden: For God knows that the day you eat thereof, your eyes shall be opened, and you shall be as Gods, knowing good and evil." Here we go again; the Gods know and do evil. And this was confirmed by God.

Genesis 3:22 says, "And the Lord God said and confirmed it, behold the man has become as one of us, to know good and evil."

When Jesus told everybody how to pray, He said, "And lead us not into temptation, but deliver us from evil." Again, Jesus knew what God was capable of doing.

However, we have to realize that good cannot exist without its opposite, evil, and vice versa, just like darkness and light. If there was no darkness, how could we call light light? Light would not have any meaning. Other examples are hot and cold, young and old, male and female, rich and poor, heaven and hell, God and the devil. This would mean God could not exist without the devil and vice versa, which is true, because if there was no devil, then everybody would live in harmony, whether there was a God or not. Those opposites were already brought up earlier in chapter 1. In one instance, God was planning on doing evil. Moses talked God out of doing this evil (Exodus 32:10). Moses had a dialogue with God, who was angry with the Israelites in the desert when He found out they had worshipped a golden calf as a God.

"And the Lord said to Moses, let me alone, so that my wrath [violent rage or fury] may wax hot again them, so that I may consume them. [Destroy them.] And I will make of you a great nation. (Exodus 32:10). Then He could start all over again with just Moses—and no female, just Moses. This could have become one more time when God was going to destroy the Israelites.

After the creation, He was ready to wipe out humankind when He found Noah. And God said, "I will never do this again—that is, wipe out everybody. But in the time of Moses, He got so ticked off He was ready to do it again—that is, destroy all the Israelites and not the whole human race this time. He had Moses to fall back on. And then like He said, He would have started with only Moses all over again—"and I will make of you a great nation."

Then Moses said to the Lord his God, "Why does your fury [wrath] wax hot against your people. Why should the Egyptians speak, and say, for mischief did He bring them out of Egypt, to slay them in the mountains, and to destroy them from the face of the earth. Turn from thy fierce wrath [violence], and repent of this evil against your people" (Exodus 32:12). Here Moses tells God what to do in no uncertain terms. Moses tells God to repent and not to do evil to the Israelites. God Himself could not see that?

Genesis 32:14 continues, "And the Lord repented of the evil which He thought to do unto his people." So, it worked. Moses could convince God not to do evil to the Israelites. Just like human beings, God does evil too, when it suits Him. This also shows that the Gods will listen to reason, if presented in a way that makes sense.

Good for Moses, he had figured out God, so it seems. And Moses shows himself to be a master salesman. Can you imagine anybody talking God out of doing something and changing His mind? Well, Moses just did! Moses made a really good and convincing point to make his plea, but God was nevertheless planning to wipe out the Israelites in spite of making the statement earlier, "I will never do that again."

Genesis 8:21 says, "I will not again curse the ground any more for man's sake, nor will I again smite every living thing as I have done." But He was planning on consuming (destroying) the Israelites anyway.

In Genesis 9:16, it says, "That I may remember the everlasting covenant between God and every living creature of all flesh upon the earth."

And God said in Genesis 9:17, "This is the token of my covenant, which I have established between me and all the flesh that is upon the earth." And now He was planning to consume all the Israelites again. How would He have done that? But Moses came to the rescue by outright telling God that He was about to make a big mistake and better change His mind.

What becomes obvious in this situation is that God definitely does not know what is going to happen beforehand. After this happened, He told Moses what had happened and ordered him to go down and leave Him alone so He could get madder against them ("So that my wrath may wax hot against them").

This indicates, for example, if a human being is dying, God does not know it either. He knows it only after death has occurred if at all, in spite of all the prayers offered for the person who is dying to no avail.

Another example is when God did not know Abel was going to die. He started to investigate after He died because He wanted to know what had happened. Yet another example is when God interrogated Adam and his woman after they had eaten from the forbidden tree. In other words, it did have to happen. God did not even know that it had happened until it was too late.

God was sorry He had anointed Saul king of Israel. Again, He did not know the outcome. Also, He did not know that the episode with the ark of Noah was futile until after it had happened, then He had to say, "I am sorry that I did, and I will never do that again!"

Genesis 8:21 says, "And the Lord said in his heart [this time He is not talking to other Gods], I will not again curse the ground any more for man's sake, neither will I again smite any more living thing, as I have done." But He had done it. From all indications, it seems He felt really bad about it. This is another human trait.

So much for the all-powerful, omnipotent God. He admits He had made a mistake of gigantic proportions by flooding the earth (Genesis 8:21) and wiping out the human race and every living being, except for just eight people and a boat with animals.

We like to look up to the Gods. We don't expect them to make mistakes, so they don't have to feel sorry later on and for whatever they did or did not. We all make mistakes, but the Gods? We make mistakes, and then we say it shows we are human. So, Gods must have human traits also? As Gods, can they not foresee what the outcome is going to be? How sad!

The powers bestowed on God are immense and without limits, beyond comprehension, because God is looked upon as an all-knowing or omniscient God. For nothing is impossible for God. You name it, and God supposedly can do it.

That's why most people are religious and need a God. They have the opportunity to petition the "Almighty" God for whatever they desire or need in life. It is their security blanket. But does He come through when needed?

A prayer is done for healing in case of sickness of oneself or one's family or anybody for that matter who needs assistance. Again, does He come through when needed? Sometimes prayer seems to work, but in the majority of prayers, it is hopeless. If or when it seems to work, then it is due to mind power, which everybody possesses. If somebody prayed for me, then God would probably say, "You want me to help that SOB? You don't know him like I do. Let him pray to me, because it is all between him and me!"

Rodeo riders do pray before the games start, so they supposedly have an advantage over the competition, which are their colleagues. Does God really care who wins a game? High school basketball teams are known to do that also, particularly Mormon teams do. It is not only basketball players but those in other sports too. The coaches and all players pray for victory. Is it so God let's His favorite team win? Or is it the most religious team?

God would have to watch every game being played—basketball, volleyball, football, golf, soccer, baseball, tennis, auto racing, Olympic games, and so on. And why not? This would explain why He can't keep up with what is going on here on earth.

Sometimes requests are answered in the positive and sometimes not. Most likely, God believes you are on your own. How convenient that is for religion. Just hope for the best.

We are told that God is an all-loving being. He loves everybody, and He will do everything if just asked with no strings attached. So, it becomes unheard of if God was not there, particularly if He is petitioned with a request for anything imaginable or needed. However, all throughout the Bible, there is no verse that says God loves us.

All our lives, we have been introduced to the all-loving God, consistently over the early years through adulthood. In the beginning, He is more like St. Nicolas. A kid can ask for anything his or her little heart desires. We tell a kid about somebody comparable to God, until he or she finds out there is no such person. Then the child is taught to replace good Old Nick with God.

God loves us so much that He gave his only begotten son (the one from a human being). Besides, He has plenty of other sons (see chapter 7), but did He in essence give His son? No, sir, only temporarily, just for a little while, then He got His son back again. However, His son had to go through a terrible ordeal, while God was doing the giving. But as we can see, He did not do much giving!

It is like if a person is fined, let's say, $25,000. It is a hardship on the person; however, if that person gets it all back in a relatively short period of time, then there is not much of a hardship for him or her at all, particularly if he or she knew that beforehand.

CHAPTER 19

Revelation Analyzed

Revelation was written by John when he had a vision, showing him supposedly what was going to happen when the world came to its end, and he was instructed to write down whatever he saw.

Now, the book of Revelation comes across as pure science fiction. Or as we would say now, it looks like John might have been on drugs.

Revelation starts out as follows. "The revelation of Jesus the Christ, which God gave to John, to show to his servants things which must shortly come to pass" (in other words, which must happen in a very short time). We are talking here about as short as two thousand years ago and still coumting.

We continue, "Blessed is he that reads it, and keeps those things which are written therein: for the time is at hand" (Revelation 1:3) (again more then two thousand years ago).

1) "He will show to his servants, things which must shortly come to pass" (Revelation 1:1).
2) "And keep those things which are written therein; for the time is at hand" (Revelation 1:3).
3) "Behold I come quickly" (Revelation 3:1).
4) "Behold I come quickly" (Revelation 22:7).
5) "And behold, I come quickly" (Revelation 22:12).

6) "Surely I come quickly" (Revelation 22:20).
7) "Sent his angel to show his servants the things which must shortly be done" (Revelation 22:6).
8) "As that the day of Christ is at hand" (2 Thessalonians 2:2).
9) Jesus himself said when still on earth: "This generation shall not pass, till all these things have been fulfilled" (Matthew 24:34).

From all indications, it definitely looks like He should have been here already. How short is "shortly"? Certainly not two thousand years. Look at how many times it has been said "shortly"!

Now, in Malachi 4:5, we read, "Behold I will send you Elijah the prophet before the coming of the great and dreadful day of the Lord, lest [in order, to prevent this from happening] I will come and smite the earth with a curse." He is still talking about the second coming of Christ. Otherwise, if not the coming of the Lord, then He "will smite the earth with a curse, which would also be a dreadful day."

What else would be the dreadful day?

Not true, because Jesus himself says, "Elias truly shall come first, and restore all things." He continues, "But I say unto you Elias is come already." Then the disciples knew He was talking about John the Baptist (Matthew 17:11– 13).

So, John the Baptist has already been here and the dreadful day of the Lord is still in limbo.

"For all the prophets and the law prophesied until John. And if he will receive it, this is Elias, who was to come." It seems a classic case of reincarnation. Elias is John the Baptist. "And Jesus asked his disciples, who do men say that I am. And they answered, John the Baptist: but some say, Elias; and others, one of the prophets." Here Jesus does not rebuke the disciples or ridicule them for bringing up reincarnation. No, it seems in those days it was understood and practiced!

Here is another example:

In John 9:1–2, it says, "And as Jesus passed by, He saw a man which was blind from his birth. And his disciples asked him, saying, Master who did sin, this man, or his parents, that he was born blind?" How can a person who is born blind sin? This is only possible if he sinned in his previous life, the life prior to being born. And the disciples knew that and asked the Master if it was him or his parents who had sinned. Jesus did not rebuke them about it this time either, because He knew about reincarnation, and it seems it was well understood.

The Messages for the Seven Churches

Now John had seven messages for the seven churches, which are only in west Asia. Those messages were strictly for the seven churches in Asia and obviously not for the rest of the world. John continues with the story of Christ's coming to earth, also meant only for the seven churches.

"Behold, He comes with clouds; and every eye shall see him." The world is round so how can every eye see Him on the other side of the world? If one lives only a few thousand miles from Asia, then there is no way one can see Him. Even Jesus was of the impression that the world was flat! I have been told that the whole world can see him through TV. However, had he come in the Middle Ages, then there would have been no way to see Christ all over the world. When He comes, that means He will be specifically coming only to western Asia, which in essence are all the countries in the vicinity of Israel and which have more or less Jerusalem at the center.

Luke 21:20–21 says, "And when you see Jerusalem compassed [more or less surrounded] with armies then you know that the desolation thereof is nigh [near]. Then let them who are in Judea flee to the mountains."

Later on, I will point out more indications of west Asia being the center of the earth, when the occasion shows up. Remember that everybody, including Jesus Himself, was of the opinion that the earth was flat.

"And they also which pierced Him and all kindred's [relatives by blood] of the earth shall wail because of Him." In the book of John, it states, "One of the soldiers with a spear pierced his side." It states specifically one soldier and not "they." There is no chance that the person who pierced Christ is still around after two thousand years, again, indicating this was supposed to have happened within a lifetime after Christ's death. Even Jesus Himself said so, as is written in Matthew 24:34, Luke 21:32, and in Mark 13:30, "Verily I say unto you, this generation shall not pass, till all these things are fulfilled." However, that generation is long gone, and all those things are not fulfilled.

Jesus is talking here about His coming again, as follows, "And they shall see the son of man coming in the clouds of heaven. And He shall send his angels, and they shall gather his elect from the four winds, from one end of heaven to the other," indicating that heaven is flat also and is not limitless, but how about the four winds? Heaven has its boundaries!

Jesus only said that, according to Matthew and Mark, not Luke. And then Jesus says, "Heaven and earth shall pass away [come to an end]." Now we are told that heaven will also pass away? Yes, in Revelation 21:1, it says so. This is what Jesus Himself proclaimed.

Now in Revelation 1:11, Jesus tells John, "I am the Alpha and Omega, the first and the last. What you see, write in a book, and send it to the seven churches which are in Asia." So, the book of Revelation was meant strictly for the seven churches again, to enlighten them in those days. And then the specific location of the churches is given.

The following reports came from John, and here we can question what he saw. John saw seven candlesticks, … and in the midst of the seven candlesticks was one like to the son of man, clothed with a garment down to the foot, and girt about the paps [breasts?] with a golden girdle. His head and his hair were white like wool, as white as snow, and his eyes were as aflame of fire; and his feet like fine brass, as if they burned in a furnace; and his voice as the sound of many waters. And he had in his right hand seven stars. And out of his mouth went a sharp two-edged sword; and his countenance [facial expression] was as the sun shines in his strength, and when I saw him, I fell at his feet as dead. And he laid his right hand upon me [the one that was holding the seven stars!] saying to me, fear not; I am the first and the last [Jesus Himself]. And I have the keys of hell and of death. Write down what you have seen.

This would mean that hell and death are locked, so that you cannot get in or out.

The mystery of the seven stars, which you saw in my right hand, and the seven candlesticks. The seven stars are the angels of the seven churches and the candlesticks are the seven churches.

Here we have an indication of the tremendous significance the seven churches had. They all had their own angels, one for each church. This whole story is woven around the seven churches in Asia at that time. And it sure does not include the Vatican.

Now the next chapter in Revelation,

To the angel of the first church (Ephasus) write; the following things say Jesus: Or else I will come to thee quickly [How quickly can he come?] and I will remove your candlestick out of his place, except you repent. [Otherwise, He will not come quickly?] ... You hate the deeds of the

Nicolaitanes, which I also hate.

Not very becoming of Jesus, He admits He hates! It is His prerogative to hate. But we don't expect that from Jesus. And He continues, "To him that overcomes will I give to eat of the tree of life, which is in the midst of the paradise of God." Why does one need the tree of life when one is already in the paradise of God? Is it that the paradise of God is different than heaven maybe?

And then Jesus gives instructions to all the seven churches. And now, beginning in chapter 4, the science fiction starts.

And he that sat on the throne was to look upon like jasper and a sardine stone [whatever that might be]: and there was a rainbow round about the throne, seen like an emerald [indicating that it rains there also, because of the rainbow]. Round the throne were twenty-four seats and I saw twenty four elders sitting, in white garments and on their heads crowns of gold. Out of the throne proceeded lightning and thundering and voices: and there were seven lamps burning before the throne, which are the seven spirits of God. And before the throne there was a sea of glass like crystal, and in the midst, and round about the throne, were four beasts full of eyes before and behind. And the first beast was like a lion, the second like a calf, and the third beast had a face like a man, and the fourth beast was like a flying eagle. And the four beasts had each of them six wings, and they were full of eyes within, and they [the animals] did not rest day and night, saying, holy, holy, Lord Almighty, which was and is, and is to come.

So now we have talking animals and weird ones to boot. The serpent in the Garden of Eden makes sense now. Can you imagine those four animals talking day and night and saying the same thing over and over! Sounds more like what robots would do. That would make an interesting but boring movie.

"And when those beasts gave glory and honor and thanks to him that sat on the throne, the twenty-four elders fell down before the one on the throne, and worshipped him, and cast their crowns of gold before the throne, saying: for thou has created all things, and for thy pleasure they are and were created." So, Adam and his woman were only created for God's pleasure!

Revelation 5:3 says, "And no man in heaven, not in earth, neither under the earth was able to open the book." Here again a reference to the earth as being flat ("neither under the earth").

Revelation 5:6 says, "And I beheld, and lo, in the midst of the throne, and (in the midst) of the four beasts, and in the midst of the elders, stood a lamb as it had been slain, having seven horns and seven eyes, which are the seven spirits of God sent forth into all the earth." So there were three lambs, one in the midst of the throne, one in the midst of the four beasts, and one in the midst of the elders. And the lamb was not in all that good shape. What an overkill! A lamb with seven horns and seven eyes, the more the better.

In Revelation 4:5, it states, "And there were seven lamps of fire burning, which are the seven Spirits of God again."

So, what are the spirits of God? Is it the lamb with seven horns and seven eyes or the seven lamps burning?

"And when he had taken the book, the four beasts and twenty-four elders fell down before the lamb, having every one of them harps." Harps and trumpets in heaven. Who was the manufacturer of those instruments? Probably they say "Made in Heaven." It would be interesting to see spirits playing instruments. Or did God say, "Let there be harps," and there they were?

We continue with this verse: "Harps and golden vials full of odors, which are the prayers of saints."

Revelation 5:11 says, "And I behold, and I heard the voice of many angels round about the throne and the four beasts and the elders."

Now it comes: "And the number of them was ten thousand times ten thousand," which is one billion, plus thousands and thousands more. It is debatable that John saw that many of them. Surely it must have looked like an impressive amount, but a billion plus? And just around the throne and the four beasts and the elders? And they were all speaking with a loud voice. Can you imagine how that would sound if a billion plus people said something with a loud voice? And a billion around the throne, the four beasts, and the elders? One could only see thousands of them. Can you picture a billion sparrows flying overhead? A couple hundred of them already look very impressive. But so be it. John counted them somehow. How does one count ten thousand angels? And then he has to count ten thousand times more angels!

Continuing, it says, "And every creature which is in heaven, and on the earth, and under the earth, and such are in the sea, and all that are in them." So, in heaven, there are creatures just like on earth.

John said, "I heard them saying, Blessing and honor, and glory, and power be to him that sits on the throne, and to the lamb." So, all the creatures in heaven and on earth and in the sea are talking, including all the fish! It would be a big surprise if all of a sudden, your dog and cat could say whole sentences, but then this is more or less science fiction.

"And when the lamb opened the first seal, I saw a white horse, and the rider had a bow and a crown was given to him and he went conquering." To conquer with bows was all they knew in John's days! Not much of a match for a machine gun or a tank or a cannon and other present-day weapons.

"And then he opened the second seal, and there was another horse that was red, and power was given to the rider to take peace from the earth, and that they should kill each other: and he was given a great sword." There is not much peace on earth so far. It's always war on earth, it seems. So, there is not much peace to take from the earth.

That was obviously impressive to John. First, in those days, the only means of transportation on land was a horse. The sword at the present time is not much of a weapon either, only if one is in man-to-man combat using swords.

"And then he opened the third seal." Now it is a black horse and the rider had a pair of balances in his hand.

"And when he had opened the fourth seal …" This time, there was a pale horse, the rider's name was death, and hell followed with him. Hell is not exactly an entity. So how does hell and everyone in it follow the horse? That must be some sight, unimaginable! "And power was given unto them over a fourth part of the earth, to kill with sword and hunger, and with death, and with the beasts of the earth."

"And when he had opened the fifth seal, John saw and he saw under the altar the souls of them that were slain for the word of God. And while they were underneath the altar they cried with a loud voice, how long O Lord before you judge and avenge our blood on them that dwell on the earth?" They were getting impatient, which is normal, considering it has been more than two thousand years they have been waiting. Weird, because those people by now are already dead. So, they don't dwell anymore on earth.

"And white robes were given to every one of them." Can you picture a soul with a robe? Why a robe? To keep them warm maybe?

"And when the sixth seal, and, lo there was a great earthquake and the sun became black and the moon become as blood." If there was an earthquake on earth, this would not turn the sun black, burned out in other words. Everyone would die, and the moon would not have any color whatsoever, as it gets its light from the sun.

"And the stars of heaven fell unto the earth, just as a fig tree discards her untimely figs, when she is shaken of a mighty wind." As I said before, they had no idea at that time what stars were. They were just pretty lights in the sky; here, they were compared to figs on a fig tree. Let's face it; even one star falling on earth would have obliterated it. But now he is talking about the stars—the stars of heaven, all of them?

"And everybody was talking to the mountains and to the rocks, and said fall on us." Since when do people talk to rocks and mountains; they are inanimate and cannot talk back, so what gives here?

Revelation 7 begins, "And after these things I [that is John] saw four angels standing on the four corners of the earth, holding the four winds of the earth, so that the wind should not blow on the earth." How does one hold the wind? Science fiction again! There are no four corners on the earth. And each angel was holding one of the four winds? Here it proves that the deities in heaven, that is God and Jesus, have no idea that the world is not flat in spite of God creating the earth. It must have been originally flat too. All planets are spheres, as we know for sure.

"Now I saw another angel descending from the east, having the seal of the living God." How does one descend from the east? East is a direction. Descent from heaven, yes, but descent from the east?

> And the angel cried with a loud voice to the four angels, standing on the four corners of the earth, saying, hurt not the earth, neither the sea, nor the trees, till we have sealed the servants of our God in their foreheads. And I heard the number of them, a hundred and forty-four thousand of all the tribes of the children of Israel.

Each tribe had twelve thousand sealed. Again, an indication of the significance of the Jews.

Here the angels are standing again on the four corners of the earth, which is pretty hard to do even for an angel. Maybe at the end of the world, Jesus will make the earth flat?

"After this I beheld, a great multitude, which no man could number." Even John could not, though he could earlier count to a billion plus. "They stood before the throne, clothed in white robes, and palms in their hands." This means that there is vegetation growing in heaven? Or artificial may be? And the billion plus angels stood around the throne, and the multitude was also standing before the throne? This must have been such an unbelievable amount of souls and angels that it boggles the mind.

Revelation 7:16 says, "They shall hunger no more, neither thirst, for the lamb which is in the midst of the throne shall feed them." Again, we are talking about souls, who don't need to be fed!

> And now He opened the seventh seal, then there was silence in heaven, for half an hour. And the seven angels, standing before God, were given each a trumpet. The first angel sounded the trumpet and there followed hail and fire mingled with blood, and it was thrown on the earth, and a

third of the trees was burnt up, and all the green grass was burnt up. And the second angel sounded, and as it were a great mountain burning with fire was thrown in the sea: and the third part of the sea became blood [makes one wonder what blood type that was, because God had an aversion to blood], and a third of the creatures in the sea died, and a third of the ships were destroyed. And the third angel sounded, and there fell a great star from heaven, burning as it were a lamp [It sounds like he saw a meteor or a comet streaking through the sky], and it fell on the third parts of the rivers, and on the fountains of water. [If a great star fell on a third of the rivers on earth, then there would not be an earth left anymore for sure.]

And the fourth angel sounded, and the third part of the sun was smitten, and the third part of the moon, and the third part of the stars. [Earlier, it was said that the sun was blacked out. That is, well, so fantastic. A third of the stars were gone? There are billions and billions of them maybe some black holes too. And a third of the sun? Everything would get out of orbit and fly off into space because of a lack of gravity. What was left of it would break up into multiple pieces.]

The fifth angel sounded, and I saw a star fall from heaven on the earth, and to him was given the key of the bottomless pit. [Who was "and to him"? Either the fifth angel or the falling star? Anyhow, he is supposedly the good angel and he opened the bottomless pit? Why? If it is bottomless, then nobody could come out of the pit anyway. No need for a lock and key. So it must be the fifth angel. And what is a bottomless pit? A pit in which there is no bottom, infinite, forever going. Or when the earth is round, then you come out at the other side of the earth? If the bottomless pit is on earth?] And he opened the bottomless pit, and smoke came out of the pit, and out of the smoke came locusts upon the earth, with power like scorpions, and the shape of the locusts were like horses, and they had crowns like gold, and their faces were like a man The sixth angel sounded and I heard a voice saying, loosen the four angels which are bound in the great river Euphrates. [Here we have again an indication that everything plays out in Asia Minor.]

And the number of the army of the horsemen were two hundred million, and John heard the number of them [so he was told this time how many]. And the heads of the horses were as the heads of lions. And they had fire and smoke coming out of their mouth. For their power is in their mouth, and in their tails, for their tails were like serpents, and they had heads, and with them they hurt.

Revelation 9 talks of tails with heads. Did John see all that? Or was he hallucinating?

And John was given a measuring tape and was told to measure the temple of God, and them that worship therein. [Must be belonging to the Jews.] But the court without a temple measure it not; for it belongs to the gentiles, and they shall tread the holy city [Jerusalem] under foot for forty-two months (Revelation 11:2).

Here is talk about the Gentiles again, the non-Jews. The Gentiles will keep Jerusalem underfoot for forty-two months, which is three and a half years. Again, Jerusalem is mentioned, so that is in Asia Minor.

"And their dead bodies shall lie in the street of the great city, which spiritually [pertaining to God] is called Sodom and Egypt, where also our Lord was crucified." How many times was He crucified? And in Sodom and Egypt as well. How strange that is!

Now on to chapter 12.

And their appeared a great wonder in heaven; a woman clothed with the sun, and the moon under her feet [must have been some sight and a great wonder], and on her head a crown of twelve stars [must have been a hell of a big crown].

And there appeared another wonder in heaven; and behold a great red dragon, having seven heads and ten horns, and seven crowns on his head. [The more the better.] And his tail drew the third part of the stars of heaven, and cast them to the earth.

This is an impossible feat no matter how big the dragon; he could not have drawn the third part of the stars of heaven and cast them to the earth. The distance in light-years makes that impossible. Imagine the third part of heaven fell on the earth by a blow from his tail. Now we know for sure that God and Jesus don't have any idea about the enormity of the stars, in spite of God claiming that He created them in the beginning. Again, there are billions and billions!

"And the woman fled into the wilderness, where she had a place prepared by god, so that they should feed her for 1260 days."

Revelation 12:7 says, "And there was war in heaven: Michael and his angels fought against the dragon; and the dragon and his angels fought. And prevailed not; neither was their place found any more in heaven," indicating that the dragon or devil do reside in heaven right now, until the time comes of the fight with Michael at the end of the world.

Revelation 13 begins,

And I stood on the sand of the sea, and saw a beast rise up out of the sea, having seven heads and ten horns, and on his horns ten crowns. And the beast was as a leopard, and his feet were as the feet of a bear, and his mouth like the mouth of a lion; and the dragon [Satan] gave him his power, and his seat, and great authority.

And I beheld another beast coming up out of the earth; and he had two horns like a lamb, and he spoke as a dragon. [How does a dragon speak?] And there follows another angel, saying, Babylon is fallen, is fallen, that great city. [Babylon was an ancient city located on the Euphrates, again in Asia Minor! But it does not exist anymore.]

And I heard a great voice say to the seven angels, go your ways and pour the vials upon the earth. And the sixth angel poured out his vial upon the great river Euphrates. [Not even the Nile, Amazon, or Mississippi. No, sir, the great river Euphrates. Again, everything is happening in Asia Minor!]

Chapter 18:2 begins, "And the angel cried with a loud voice, saying Babylon the great city is fallen." Observe nothing so far has happened outside Asia Minor.

Revelation 18:8 says, "Therefore shall her plagues come in one day, death, and mourning, and a famine." How can there be famine in one day? Starvation in one day? One can easily survive one day without food.

Revelation 18:10 says, "Alas, that great city Babylon, that mighty city for in one hour your judgment comes."

Revelation 18:21 states, "Thus with violence shall that great city Babylon be thrown down, and shall be no more at all."

And in Revelation 19:17, we read, "And I saw an angel standing in the sun." Angels can do that probably. But it is not very cool, literally! But it was said earlier that the sun was black.

Revelation 9:11 reads, "And they had a king, which is the angel of the bottomless pit. Whose name in the Hebrew language is Abaddon." This must have been a bad angel. In verse 1, it states that one of the good angels was given the keys to the bottomless pit.

Revelation 21:1 says, "And I saw a new heaven and a new earth: for the first heaven and earth were passed away; and there was no more sea. Makes one wonder if there really was a new heaven and a new earth? And if the earth was flat again, then everybody in the old heaven was eliminated?

Revelation 21:2 says, "And I John saw the holy city, New Jerusalem coming down from God out of heaven," and again in Revelation 21:10, "And He carried me away and showed me that great city, the holy Jerusalem, descending out of heaven from God. And it had twelve gates and names written thereon, which are the names of the twelve tribes of the children of Israel." Here we see again that the whole story about the coming of Christ centers on the Jews and Israel. And when the time comes, with all the animals and plagues and the fighting, then you better not be in Asia Minor, because all hell will break loose there. And only the good Jews will be saved. But we non-Jews will all be wiped out supposedly, which includes all the Christians.

In conclusion, everything happening indicates Asia Minor is the area where all the dreadful things are going to happen. References are made all through Revelation to that area, like the city of Babylon, the river Euphrates, Judea, Jerusalem, and the new holy Jerusalem, which replaces the old Jerusalem. And at the end, it states it had a wall, great and high, with twelve gates and names written thereon, which are the names of the twelve tribes of Israel. This shows that God's only concern is still for the Jews. He definitely does not need Gentiles. And He will supposedly always help the Jews, with whom He made pacts and covenants since day 1.

In John 4:22, Jesus Himself says, "For salvation is of the Jews." And again, in Acts 11:19, we read, "Stephen travelled as far as Phoenicia, and Cyprus, and Antioch, preaching the word to none but unto the Jews only."

Why does the new city of Jerusalem need a wall and gates? Is it to keep the enemy out? Or does this refer to the olden days when every city of importance was fortified?

Reverence is made more than once to the great river Euphrates, but no mention is ever made of the greatest river, the Nile, just to stay in the general vicinity. The Euphrates ranks in size as the twenty-seventh largest river in the world. So, it's not all that great a river, being that twenty-six rivers are greater than the Euphrates. But the river is in Asia Minor, where everything plays out at the end.

And Jesus says that the earth is flat while his angels are standing on the four corners of the earth, each one holding one of the four winds. Again, He does not know that the world is a globe?

In Mark 13:27, Jesus Himself said this, "And he shall gather together his elect from the four winds, from the uttermost part of the earth." There can only be an uttermost part of the world if it is flat. What a surprise He will have when He comes back for His second coming here on earth and discovers that the world is round—if he ever comes.

And John was capable of seeing in one glance a conglomeration of a billion plus angels?

The bottom line is we in the United States don't have to worry much about Christ's second coming. From all indications, everything is going to happen in the east.

I heard a preacher tell his followers (on a radio broadcast) that if it appears the world is coming to its end, then the best place to be is in Israel! Weird!

CHAPTER 20

The Missing Books and Other Weird Things

The Bible is supposed to be the word of God. Why is it then that some books, originated by God, are missing, left out, destroyed or whatever—they are not there. See for yourself.

Josh.10:13 says, "The sun stood still, and the moon stayed until the people had avenged themselves upon their enemy; is this not written in the book of Jasher?" The sun is always in a stationary position in relation to earth. So, this should have been, "And the earth stood still and the moon stood still!" But as mentioned earlier, nobody knew that the earth was round in those days and everybody was under the impression that the earth was also still the center of the universe! Where is this book of Jasher? Was something in there not liked or disagreeable?

Here we go again. "And David lamented with his lamentation over Saul and over Jonathan his son. Also, he bade them to teach the children of Judah the use of the bow: 'Behold it is written in the book of Jasher'" (2 Samuel 1:18). Again, where is that book of Jasher?

In 2 Chronicles 13:23, we read, "And his sayings are written in the book of the prophet Iddo." And 2 Chronicles 13:15 says, "Now the acts of Rehoboam, first and last, are they not written in the book of Shemaiah the prophet and of Iddo the seer concerning genealogies?"

Who knows how many more Bible books are missing or taken out of the Bible?

Another interesting part is that Jesus was not born in December. For one, there are no shepherds in the field in December in Israel. What happened was the first pope after Peter did not like that the holidays from the heathens got quite a bit of attention and were celebrated to a great extent. The solstice (December 21) and the old and new year (December 31 and January 1) were celebrated extensively. So, he wanted Christ's birthday moved to between those holidays so the holidays would more or less coincide.

To prove that those religious days are not all that authentic, here are some other holidays: Easter was not an exact day either. Easter is celebrated on the Sunday immediately after the first full moon that occurs on or after March 21. March 21 is the start of spring. *Eastre* is the name of the Goddess of spring. And forty days after Easter is the day that commemorates Christ going to heaven, which is Ascension Day.

In 2 Kings 8:17, 20, we read, "And Jehoram, the son of Jehoshaphat king of Judah began to reign. Thirty-two years old he was, and he reigned eight years ... And he died when he was forty years old.

In 2 Kings 8:25, the statement is made that Jehoram's son, Ahaziah, was twenty-two years old when he started his reign, and he reigned one year. In 2 Chronicles 22:2, it states that Ahaziah was forty-two years old when he began his reign and he reigned one year. We know already that Jehoram died when he was forty years old, and his son Ahaziah started to reign in succession when he was forty-two years old. This indicates that his son was older than his father!

In 1 Kings 16:5–8 is recorded the death of Baasha in the twenty-sixth year of the reign of Asa, King of Judah. Now in 2 Chronicles 16:1, we have here a contradiction; Asa Baasah, king of Israel, came up against Judah in the thirty- sixth year of his reign. This made it ten years after Baashah's death.

However, this is small stuff and insignificant. It is more or less nitpicking, concerning those last two paragraphs. This does not make any difference to the Bible's authenticity whatsoever! It's just a screwup.

Now observe in Luke 3:23, it is written "And Jesus himself began to be about thirty years of age [being as was supposed to be], the son of Joseph, which was the son of Heli," and so forth all the way down to Adam, and Adam was supposed to be, as it says, the son of God. Not exactly much of a son to be proud of, if He ever was. Besides that, Adam was first created by God in His image, just Adam alone, and later Adam was again created, this time by the Lord. Now the Lord made Adam out of the dust of the ground from scratch again. If Adam was a son of God, he must have had a lot of God's DNA, but then the Lord had to create him again out of dust.

What happened to Jesus after He was twelve years old? That was the last time He was mentioned in the Bible until He came back when He was thirty years old, as mentioned again in the New Testament. Eighteen years are missing of Jesus's life. There are records and references in Tibet and Egypt that He was there and He was also in India!

However, as was mentioned earlier, Jesus was the son of Joseph and not God.

Now, in Luke 4:22, it states, "And a voice came from heaven, which said, you are my beloved Son; in you I am well pleased." So, does this indicate that Jesus became God's son at the time of him being baptized? If Adam was a son of God, then God loved Jesus more than anyone else, besides his sons, as mentioned in an earlier chapter. He made Him His beloved son. That is nice, but fathers here on earth are supposed to love all their children evenly, and generally they do. And if Adam was God's son, then how could

God offer up His only begotten son? Again, why are Adam's and God's sons mentioned in Genesis. Just to do us a favor?

John 1:45 says, "We have found him, of whom Moses in the law, and the prophets, did write, Jesus of Nazareth, the son of Joseph." Again, Joseph here, according to the Bible, is the father of Jesus. Misprints maybe?

Luke 4:12 says, "And Jesus answering said to him, you shall not tempt the lord your God." However, God can and will tempt us, as proven in the Lord's Prayer: "Lead us not in to temptation, but deliver us from evil." This is what he taught us to pray!

However, in Deuteronomy 7:15, God talks here about the evil diseases He put on the Egyptians, which were the ten plagues! He did evil, He admits, by putting those evil plagues on the Egyptians.

In 2 Kings 21:12, it says, "Therefore said the Lord, behold I am bringing such evil upon Jerusalem and Judah, that whosoever hears of it, both his ears will tingle." It definitely looks like God enjoys doing evil!

Isaiah 45:7 says, "I form the light and I create darkness." How? By getting rid of the light? He continues, "I make peace, and I create evil, I the Lord do all those things." By now we do know for sure that He likes to create evil! He Himself proclaimed it!

In 1 Corinthians 13:13, it says, "And now abide faith, hope and charity. These three; but the greatest of these is charity." Charity is better than faith? So, if you don't have faith, then don't feel bad as long as you have charity. This is Paul speaking. He says other weird things.

In 1 Corinthians 11:7–9, he says, "Forasmuch as a man is in the image and glory of God: but the woman is the glory of man." Thus, the woman is not in God's image. "Neither was the man created for the woman: but the woman was created for the man." This is Paul speaking. Paul supposedly knows all this, because he was never married himself.

In the twelfth century, there was a bishop by the name of St. Malachias, who predicted that the year 2021 would be the year that the last pope would reign; there would be one more pope after this pope and then the Roman Catholic Church would be gone.

Now observe the first verse in this chapter, Joshua 10:13, "And the sun stood still and the moon stayed until the people had avenged themselves upon their enemy."

How strange! God did not know that the sun is always standing stationary in the universe and the earth revolves in orbit around the sun. So, the all-knowing God does not know that the earth orbits the sun? He supposedly did create the earth and the sun and the universe Himself!

Again, in the olden days, everybody thought for sure that the earth was flat and was the center of the universe. It would have been very impressive if He had said, "And the earth stood still"! But no, it seems He wanted to patronize everybody. But in essence, He was telling something He was not aware of.

There are over fifty references in the Bible and in the New Testament about the sun rising or setting, too many to list here. It would become too monotonous to show them all here. However, God and Jesus each mention at times that the sun rises and sets, but we use this still today too. So, it could be a matter of speech. It would have made more sense if they had called it "daybreak" or "day set." It is still customary in our society and all over the world for that matter. For example, the motor vehicle department states, "Turn on your headlights half an hour after sun down." So, it is still what we see in our daily observations. But it proves that God and Jesus had no idea that the world is round.

We keep most of the Ten Commandments, but the one about the Sabbath is completely ignored, except by the Jews. And it seems we are getting away with it too! But now the moon comes about, which should be just as holy as the Sabbath. God describes the moon as holy as the Sabbath.

In 2 Corinthians 8:13–14, it says, "This according to Solomon: offering according to the commandments of Moses, on the Sabbaths, and on the new moons, and on the solemn feasts."

In 2 Corinthians 31:3, it says, "For the morning and the evening burnt offerings, and the burnt offerings for the Sabbaths, and for the new moons, and for the set feasts, as it is written in the law of the Lord."

Ezra 3:5 states, "They kept also the feast of the tabernacles, as it is written. And afterwards offered the continual burnt offering, both of the new moons, and of all the set feasts of the Lord that were consecrated."

Nehemiah 10:33 says, "For the showbread, and for the continual meat offering, of the Sabbath, of the new moons, for the set feasts, and for the holy things."

Ezekiel 45:17 says, "And it shall be the prince's part to give burnt offerings, and meat offerings, and drink offerings, in the feasts, and in the new moons, and in the Sabbaths, in all solemnities of the house."

Ezekiel 46:3 says, "Likewise the people of the land shall worship at the door of this gate before the Lord in the Sabbaths and in the new moons."

In 1 Samuel 20:18, it says, "Jonathan said to David tomorrow is the new moon, and you will be missed, because your seat will be empty."

In 1 Samuel 20:24, it says, David hid himself in the field, and when the new moon had come, the king sat him down to eat."

Ezekiel 46:6 says, "And in the day of the new moon the offering shall be a young bullock without blemish."

So, from all indications, the new moon was always celebrated like the Sabbath and honored by giving offerings. So, in the following texts, we find a contradiction!

Isaiah 2:13 says, "However the Lord said: 'bring no more vain oblations; incense is an abomination to me; the new moons and Sabbaths, it is iniquity.'" (*Iniquity* is sin.)

Now the Sabbath is also an iniquity or a sin? How strange after making observation of the Sabbath one of the Ten Commandments.

Isaiah 2:14 says, "Your new moon, and your appointed feasts my soul hates: they are a trouble unto me." Now even the feasts and the new moon God hates. The Passover is also an appointed feast, which He hates also. Strange.

Psalm 104:19 says, "He appointed the moon for seasons: and the sun knows his going down."

So, the moon is for seasons. What seasons? The moon is always there and in kind of a predictable way, but it also varies from season to season.

CHAPTER 21

The Trinity

Most Christian denominations believe in the Trinity. Catholics, as well as most Protestants, go for it and believe in it.

The Trinity, however, is never mentioned in the Old Testament and never even mentioned by God. It never appears in the New Testament either, not spoken of by Jesus or the apostles. Not even once in the whole Bible is there a statement that there is a trinity! Because it is all fabricated by human beings.

Then why do the Christians live by it? It sounds nice and would make a lot of sense if it was so. But how did it come about?

It was made up by the first pope after the death of Christ (the church states that Peter was the first one, so it was the next pope). Now, if we look at how this pope lived and reigned as a pope, we don't get too nice a picture. For instance, he envied his brother because he liked his brother's wife and he had his brother killed so he could have his wife. He also gave orders to the monks to change words or sentences in the original biblical manuscripts so that they complied more with the line of thinking of the church. Those documents can still be seen as the original corrected documents, as they exist to this day with the changed notations in the margins at the cathedral in what used to be Constantinople. (This looks amazingly the same as what happens in the present time, when changes are made throughout the Bible and implanted in the new

Bibles, such as the New English Bible or the New International Version, to name a couple.)

Well, as the story goes, this pope told the heathen peoples—the Greeks, the Italians, the Egyptians, the Indians, and other surrounding populations—they had too many Gods. There was Zeus, Neptune, Prometheus, and Apollo just to name a few.

They replied, "Look at yourself. You have three Gods—God, the Son, and the Holy Spirit."

He had to admit that there were in essence three Gods, and he came out with an edict that henceforth all three would be considered as one; thus came the Trinity into existence, a man-made invention originated by the Catholic Church.

This was agreed upon at the Nicene Council of AD 325 and was reconfirmed more than fifty-five years later at the Second Council of Constantinople in AD 381, after which it became the standard of the orthodox teachings.

This is what they came up with:

We believe in God the Father Almighty, maker of heaven and earth and of all things visible and invisible, and in one Lord Jesus Christ, the only begotten son of God, begotten of the Father before all worlds, God of God, Light of Light, very God of very God, begotten, not made, being of one substance with the Father, by whom all things were made and in the holy spirit, the Lord and giver of life, who proceeds from the Father and the Son.

This is a beautiful creed as far as the churches are concerned, for both the Catholic and Protestant religions, in spite of being man-made and over fifty years in the making. Controversy over this creed arose, and around six hundred years later, the Eastern Orthodox Church broke away from Western Christendom. They proclaimed that the Holy Spirit was not a body like the father and the son were.

In the seventeenth century, there was again a controversy, revived by Faustus Socinus, an Italian theologian who organized an anti-Trinitarian movement. Force was used to repress this movement, and many were killed on the orders of the church. Nevertheless, this movement and its influence spread to Poland, Germany, Holland, and later to England and from there to North America, mainly Canada, in the nineteenth century. It caused a division of the churches and resulted in the rise of the Unitarian denomination.

The majority of the churches did cling to the Trinitarian faith, and it is the keystone of Christianity—even if it was man-made.

That the Trinity does not make much sense becomes clearer when we look at the following:

- Mark 13:32—Here, Jesus Himself makes the statement "neither the so the angels but the father knows." He does not mention the Holy Ghost. This is when the end of the world begins. So here the father keeps this from his son. In spite of them supposedly being one.
- Luke 23:34—"Then Jesus asks, 'Father forgive them, for they know not they are doing.'" He had to ask the father; this means that He cannot forgive sins Himself! He cannot forgive sins? Then this means that only the father can forgive sins.
- Luke 22:42—Jesus went to the Mount of Olives and prayed, "Father, if be willing, remove this cup from me: never the less not my will but you done." Jesus here asked (begged) God three times, but to no avail. should He? He had no mercy on Job either when He made the deals with Satan.

Well, it sure looks like there are two different entities talking to each other. God did not even bother to give Jesus an answer. He sent an angel who had mercy on Him and gave Him comfort.

Why did God not bother to give Him support? It becomes obvious God had His plan and He wanted His plan executed His way only, in spite of Jesus having to go through a terrible ordeal.

Jesus could heal people and raise people from the dead. Therefore, we could also assume that He would not feel pain anytime when He did not want to feel pain, like during the crucifixion.

Now, in Revelation 1:4, it says, "Grace be unto you, and peace, from him which is and which was, and which is to come; and from the seven spirits which are before his throne; And from Jesus Christ" and so on.

Now in Revelation 5:6, we again get a whole different picture about the seven spirits. Here, it says, "And in the midst of the elders, stood a lamb as it had been slain, having seven horns and seven eyes, which are the seven spirits of God. Those spirits are the seven horns and seven eyes."

First, there were seven candles burning before the throne, and those were the seven spirits of God; then there was a lamb that had seven horns and seven eyes, which were the seven spirits of God. Nice going. Who can explain this? Leave it up to the people who write biblical commentaries, because they can explain everything even in the weirdest ways.

In Genesis 1, it says, "And the spirit of God flew over the uncreated earth." This must be the Holy Spirit. Was He making reconnaissance flights maybe? This Spirit certainly would make more sense than the seven candles.

There is no reference in the Bible anywhere to Jesus and the Holy Ghost having been one at any given time. It is His spirit that keeps Him going—just like human beings, who possess spirits and souls.

CONCLUSION

What follows is, I think, a marvelous statement made by Gotthold Lessing in his book *Anti-Gotze*.

The true value of a man is not determined by his possession, supposed or real, or Truth, but rather by his sincere exertion to get to the truth. It is not possession of the truth but rather the pursuit of truth by which he extends his powers and in which his ever growing perfectibility is to be found. Possession makes one passive, indolent, and proud.

So far, we can conclude the following:

- We worship a God who is jealous.
- We worship a God who hates.
- We have Gods who said, "Now that they have become like one of us, now know good and evil."
- We worship a God who is sorry about all the mistakes He made.
- We worship a God who said, "I do good, and I create evil."
- We worship a God who does not know what is going on at critical times.
- We worship a God who makes all kinds of covenants with the Jews only supposedly for eternity, but was not willing to help them when they were dying in concentration camps.
- We have a God who likes the smell of meat and has no use for produce offered to Him.

- We have a God who promises us anything if we just ask but does no attention to us even if we beg. Jesus Himself begged three times to have cup removed but to no avail.
- We have a Lord who hates foreign or strange Gods with a passion doesn't want to hear about them. He will kill you if you pay any attention to them.
- We have a God who sent bears to kill the children who teased the prophet Elisha because he was bald and Elisha complained to God not about baldness but about the teasing.
- We have a Lord who likes to tempt us whenever He feels the need. Himself taught the Lord's Prayer, in which He said, "Lead us not into temptation."
- We have a Lord who is not omnipotent and omniscient. For instance, He did not know that Adam was going to fail Him by eating the forbidden fruit that has caused quite a commotion up to this day.
- We have a God who repented that He had made man on earth, and it grieves Him at His heart, but when He created man, it was very good.
- When God created heaven and earth, He was not aware that He had some time, to create a hell also. God wiped out everything in a flood. He felt sorry afterward.
- We have a God who threatened to wipe out all the Israelites while they in the desert when He found out that they had worshipped a golden calf did not anticipate that either.
- We have a God who was curious and had to see what Adam would call an animal. He obviously had no idea what Adam would call them.

All the aforementioned idiosyncrasies ascribed to God are almost the same as what humans would and can do. Because we were created in His image?

One of my brothers in law asked me once; did God create men, or did men create God?

These Gods are either Elohim or Jahweh—in other words, God or the Lord God. In previous chapters, I have shown them to be two distinct and different Gods. At times, they interfered with each other, but in spite of it, they always tolerate each other.

"Know thyself" was inscribed on the temple of Delphi in Greece. This is a basic principle, but have we learned to do that? Do we know ourselves?

Well, by going through the Bible, I have located all kinds of discrepancies and contradictions. There are in all probability more of them. But at least I did read the Bible to some extent.

Where are all the people who profess to have read the Bible from A to Z and more than once but never observed all the idiosyncrasies staring them in the face? And they never reported them? If they did notice them, then they won't mention them or even talk about them. Just not to annoy God? So, they are good Christians when they read the Bible but do not question anything?

Now, one more point of interest. God, at all times, supposedly keeps track of more than six billion human beings on earth and their well-being. He has to keep an eye on the sick, the healthy, and the dying. He is supposed to know who died. He has to listen to all the constant prayers going up to Him and keep track of all the hair on human heads. As Jesus Himself said in Luke 21:18, "But there shall not a hair of your head perish and all the hairs on your head are all numbered" (KJ). "Even all the hairs on your head are counted" (Matthew 10:30 DC).

Now, He also has to keep track of the numbered hairs on your head to see if there is a hair missing. He obviously gets a break from all the ones who are bald.

So, if He spent only one second per person, then in one year, He would have looked at only 531,536,000 people out of 6 billion, and that is in one whole year. Or, for that matter, He could look at only 4,320 people in a twelve-hour day. It would take God ten thousand years to look at about 6 billion, which is everybody on earth. Now, if He spent 1/100 of a second on each person, He would still need one hundred years to look only once at everybody on earth. Then we have to add and take into consideration all the planets and all the animals He has to keep track of also. But we expect Him to keep track of us at any moment? When Adam sinned, God came looking for him but could not find him in the Garden of Eden. So how do you expect, then, that He can locate one of us out of 6 billion individuals in the whole wide world?

Besides that, He also has to keep track of the universe, which is in constant turmoil by itself. Planets do crash, which causes complete annihilation, and new stars are being born constantly, all this according to NASA.

God also has to keep track of each and every animal. As it is stated in Matthew 10:29 "Are not two sparrows sold? Yet not one of them shall fall to the ground without the will of our heavenly father."

So now it becomes more improbable for God to be capable of keeping an eye on every human being, billions of them; every animal, also billions and billions of them; every planet, of which there are billions and billions also; and also, every comet and asteroid, all of them at any time.

No wonder He definitely could not have any idea of who is going to die at any time. No wonder six million Jews went to the gas chambers without interference by God. It seems He skipped all of them or missed them all.

We are told by every denomination that our savior is Jesus the Christ. But is He? Read Isaiah 43:11. Here it says, **"I, I am the lord besides me there is no savior."** Well, the Lord knows best.

God is being worshipped as a deity who has never been seen or heard of, except as told in the Old Testament? It was written thousands of years ago while the earth has been in existence for millions and millions of years. But everybody has been conditioned and told to believe it, regardless of the facts. He is a God of whom we supposedly can ask anything we need. All we have to do is pray and ask! Not too many prayers are answered. And if there is a positive result, it is because of our minds. The mind is unbelievably powerful. Even the Reverend Osteen proclaimed on TV, "There is a great power within you." He is right, but it seems he does not realize it is the power of the mind that is available for you. Even Jesus said, "There will come after me, who can do greater things than me." This can only be done through mind power, not prayer!

I am definitely not a theologian. But I have been capable of making logical deductions and pinpointing the fallacies in the Bible. So let us leave it at that. And after reading all the data in this booklet, you can become the proverbial ostrich who sticks its head in the sand, and then you don't have to see any contradictions in the Bible.

Why did God give conflicting commands to Noah?

Why did John tell us, "Nobody has seen God," when the Bible tells us more than ninety-five people have seen God?

Revelation tells us Satan is still in heaven until the end of the world.